Recipes of Note

A Collection of Recipes from the Greensboro Symphony Guild

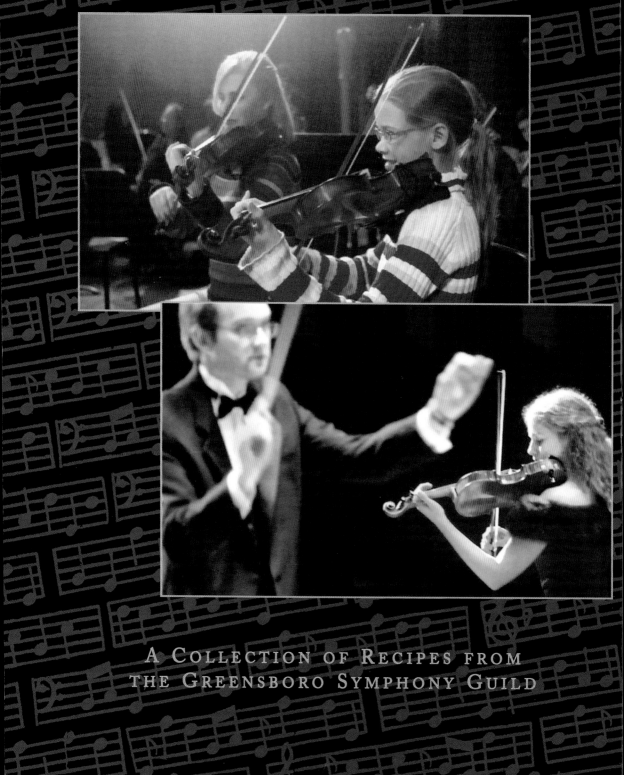

A COLLECTION OF RECIPES FROM
THE GREENSBORO SYMPHONY GUILD

Recipes of Note

Recipes of Note

A COLLECTION OF RECIPES FROM
THE GREENSBORO SYMPHONY GUILD

Published by Greensboro Symphony Guild
P.O. Box 29224, Greensboro, North Carolina 27429-9224
www.gsoguild.org

FRONT COVER: artist Christine Taylor "Parlor Music"
BACK COVER: drawing by Maggie Fickett
TITLE PAGE: photos submitted by Greensboro Symphony Orchestra
and Joseph Rodriguez, *Greensboro News and Record*
DUETS: Greensboro Symphony Guild 2005/2006 yearbook cover
PRELUDES: painting by Cotten Moring
INTERLUDES: photos submitted by Greensboro Symphony Orchestra
ACCOMPANIMENTS: artist Christine Taylor "Parlor Music"
MASTERWORKS: drawing by Maggie Fickett
ENCORES: drawing by Austine Twyman

ISBN: 0 9778390-0-1

Edited, Designed, and Manufactured by

CommunityClassics™

An imprint of

FRP™

P. O. Box 305142
Nashville, Tennessee 37230
800-358-0560

Manufactured in China
First Printing: 2006
8,000 copies

Cookbook Committee

Co-Chairs

Susan Bohn
Barbara Hemphill

Section Editors

Carol Andresen	*Brenda Barnes*	*Peggy Follin*
Martha Siler	*Ellen Taft*	*Suzy Walker*

Design Committee

Valerie Sutton, Chair   *Donna Richardson*   *Gwen Varsamis*

The Cookbook Committee is grateful to all Guild members who helped develop, design, and publish this collection of recipes. Many hours were spent preparing recipes for submission, reviewing them for selection, testing, tasting, and proofreading. In addition, there were those who graciously offered their homes for tastings all along the way. The committee sincerely thanks the creative, talented, and dedicated volunteers who have made this cookbook a reality.

Special thanks go to Marilyn Cotten, who submitted the title *Recipes of Note,* and to Gwen Varsamis, who helped with the title page concept.

Table of Contents

Duets

Appetizers & Beverages

Preludes

Breakfast, Brunch & Breads

Interludes

Soups & Salads

Accompaniments

Vegetables & Sides

115

Masterworks

Meats, Poultry & Seafood

165

Encores

Desserts

231

Preface

Wherever Guild members gather, there is always good food and fellowship—
fostering congeniality and opportunities to make lifelong friendships.
This communion provides the centerpiece for the Guild's purpose,
focus, and intent. As a support beam of the Greensboro Symphony Orchestra
and its music education programs, the Guild has accepted the responsibility
for fund-raising to ensure the ongoing gift of music in this community
and the surrounding area. Therefore, when the Guild began to evaluate
current fund-raisers, the addition of a cookbook seemed to provide
a fine blend of the Guild membership's love of tasty fare and the desire
for an additional project. Thus, *Recipes of Note* was born.
Our cookbook represents a true labor of love—one that resulted in
Guild-inspired camaraderie every step of the way—
and features many Guild talents from graphic design to the creation
of fine art and food. The Guild hopes that you will enjoy the recipes
included in this collection. They represent the collective effort
and support of many Guild members who have contributed to this project.
We are committed to dedicating the volunteer services necessary to ensure
that generations to come will benefit from the powerful influence
of live symphonic music. Won't you join us in an effort to weave
the gift of music into the fabric of our community?
You can be part of making this dream come true and share a taste
of Guild hospitality when you help yourself to a copy
of this wonderful cookbook! Bon appétit!

Mission Statement

The Greensboro Symphony Guild serves as an advocate
for music education and appreciation in the community,
primarily by supporting the Greensboro Symphony Orchestra, Inc.,
through financial, educational, and promotional activities.

GSG History/Time Line

THE GREENSBORO SYMPHONY GUILD'S MORE THAN 40 YEARS
OF SERVICE TO THE GREENSBORO SYMPHONY ORCHESTRA

1964 With eighteen charter members, the Greensboro Symphony Guild was created with assistance from the Junior League of Greensboro as a support group for the Greensboro Symphony Orchestra. The newly formed organization developed and located funding for in-school concerts performed by orchestra ensembles. Starting in 1964, the Guild developed ticket sales campaigns, secured special contributions, sold playbill ads, and worked in the United Arts Council Fund Drive, thus helping to ensure local funding for the orchestra. The Guild performed these services for the orchestra for many years.

1970–71 The Youth Orchestra was created—a collaborative effort of the Greensboro Symphony Orchestra and the Guild.

1978–88 The Guild sponsored and implemented pre-concert education programs for elementary school students with a Bert and Ernie puppet show until 1987 and with videos and booklets until 1988.

1985–94 The Guild sponsored and implemented community children's concerts, which then became family concerts.

1985 President Ronald Reagan presented the Guild with The President's Volunteer Action Award for outstanding service related to its education programs.

1986   The Guild established the Endowment Fund with a commitment to endow the $250,000 Concertmaster's Chair. This chair was fully funded in 1995.

1988   The Youth Orchestra performed at the Lincoln Center's Alice Tully Hall. The Guild continues to provide generous support for the GSYO through scholarships, awards, receptions, and funding for special events.

2001   The Guild contributed to the funding of the Associate Concertmaster's Chair. This chair was completely funded in 2004, with additional contributions from the Endowment and GSO Boards, the Guild, and community members.

The Youth Orchestra performed at the Kennedy Center's Millennium Center, with financial assistance from the Guild.

2004   The Guild received a Silver Award from the American Symphony Orchestra League for its work in the membership area.

2005   The Guild received a Silver Award from the American Symphony Orchestra League for its Golf Classic; it also received an Excellence in Innovation Award, one of only two in the nation, for its work in the newly formed marketing area.

The Guild continues to provide both financial and volunteer assistance to the Greensboro Symphony Orchestra as a result of its various fund-raising initiatives, its ongoing support of education programs, and its individual and collective commitment to ensure the future of the orchestra.

Plato

Education in music is most sovereign,
because more than anything else, rhythm and harmony
find their way to the inmost soul and take strongest hold upon it,
bringing with them an imparting grace,
if one is rightly trained.

Music is a moral law. It gives soul to the universe,
wings to the mind, flight to the imagination,
a charm to gaiety, and life to everything.
It is the essence of order, and leads to all
that is just and beautiful.

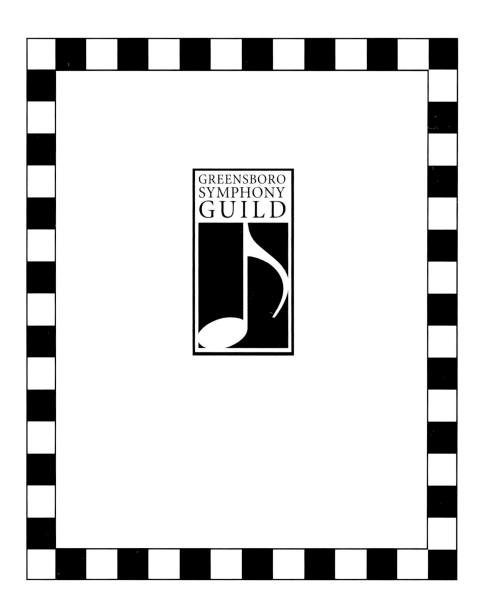

GREENSBORO
SYMPHONY
GUILD

Duets

Appetizers & Beverages

The Greensboro Symphony Guild

The Greensboro Symphony Guild was created in 1964 to promote and foster music culture and education, primarily by aiding the Greensboro Symphony Society in the promotion of an orchestra in the community. Although the antecedents of the Symphony had been performing since 1920, the Symphony Society, founded in 1959, soon recognized the need for a vital support group. With help and advice from UNCG (University of North Carolina at Greensboro) faculty members, the Junior League of Greensboro was enlisted to organize a community-based Symphony Guild of dedicated women. The Guild has grown and flourished. Almost five hundred members strong, the organization remains dedicated to the well-being of Greensboro's orchestra and to the cause of music education.

Through the years, Guild ticket campaigns, educational programs, and fund-raising efforts have received national recognition and awards from the American Symphony Orchestra League. The Guild received its greatest honor in 1985, when President Ronald Reagan bestowed upon the Guild The President's Volunteer Action Award for outstanding service.

Tequila-Marinated Shrimp

1/4 cup olive oil
3 tablespoons finely chopped onion
5 garlic cloves, chopped
2 pounds fresh peeled shrimp
1/4 cup tequila
1/4 cup lime juice
1/8 teaspoon salt
2 tablespoons chopped fresh cilantro

Heat the olive oil in a large skillet over medium heat. Add the onion and garlic and sauté for 3 minutes or until tender. Add the shrimp and tequila and bring to a boil. Simmer for 3 to 5 minutes or just until the shrimp turn pink, stirring occasionally. Remove the shrimp mixture to a bowl. Add the lime juice, salt and cilantro and toss well. Chill, covered, for 2 hours to 24 hours, stirring occasionally. Drain before serving.

Serves 10 to 12

Folly Pickled Shrimp

6 cups salted water
2 pounds fresh deveined peeled shrimp with tails
1/2 cup sugar
1 1/2 cups white vinegar
1 cup vegetable oil
1/2 cup capers, undrained
1 teaspoon salt
1 teaspoon celery seeds
1 white onion or red onion, sliced and separated into rings

Bring the water to a boil in a saucepan. Add the shrimp and cook for 3 minutes or until the shrimp turn pink. Drain and rinse in cold water. Chill until cold. Whisk the sugar, vinegar, oil, capers, salt and celery seeds in a large bowl. Add the shrimp and onion in alternating layers. Chill, covered, for 6 hours to overnight, stirring frequently. Drain and discard the marinade.

You may use frozen cooked shrimp with tails if fresh shrimp are not available. Thaw the shrimp before marinating.

Serves 10

Shrimp Tarts

FILLING
2 pounds fresh unpeeled shrimp
2/3 cup finely chopped green onions
1/2 cup finely chopped fresh parsley
2/3 cup mayonnaise
2 tablespoons rinsed and drained capers
1 teaspoon lemon juice
1/2 teaspoon salt
1/4 teaspoon cayenne pepper
1 garlic clove, minced

SHELLS
1/2 cup (1 stick) butter, softened
4 ounces cream cheese, softened
11/4 cups all-purpose flour
1/4 cup (1 ounce) grated asiago cheese
1/4 teaspoon salt

For the filling, cook the shrimp in a saucepan of boiling seasoned water until the shrimp turn pink. Drain and place in a bowl. Chill, covered, until cold. Peel, devein and coarsely chop the shrimp. Combine the shrimp, green onions, parsley, mayonnaise, capers, lemon juice, salt, cayenne pepper and garlic in a bowl and mix well. Chill, covered, until ready to fill the shells.

For the shells, beat the butter and cream cheese in a bowl until smooth. Add the flour, asiago cheese and salt and mix well. Chill, covered, for 1 hour to overnight. Divide the dough into 3 portions. Shape each portion into 12 balls. Press over the bottom and up the side of 36 lightly greased miniature muffin cups. Bake at 350 degrees for 15 to 17 minutes or until golden brown. Cool in the pans and remove to a serving plate. Spoon equal portions of the filling into the baked shells. Garnish with diagonal slices of green onions and serve immediately. The baked tart shells may be frozen after baking. Thaw before filling. Chicken salad or crab salad also makes a good filling for the shells.

Serves 18

Prosciutto-Wrapped Greens

3 tablespoons extra-virgin olive oil
2 teaspoons red wine vinegar
2 teaspoons fresh lemon juice
1/2 teaspoon Dijon mustard
4 ounces arugula and/or romaine
2 tablespoons freshly grated Parmigiano-Reggiano cheese
Salt and freshly ground pepper to taste
12 thin slices prosciutto

Whisk the olive oil, vinegar, lemon juice and Dijon mustard in a small bowl. Combine the arugula and cheese in a bowl. Add just enough of the olive oil mixture to lightly coat and toss gently. Season with salt and pepper. Lay 1 prosciutto slice on a work surface. Place a handful of the arugula mixture over the narrow end and roll up tightly. Repeat to use the remaining prosciutto and arugula mixture. Cut the rolls diagonally into 2-inch pieces. Serve alone, as part of an antipasto plate or with a mound of dressed salad greens garnished with grated cheese.

Serves 8

Prosciutto and Artichoke Wraps

1 teaspoon extra-virgin olive oil
1/2 cup (2 ounces) slivered blanched almonds
1 (14-ounce) can artichoke hearts, drained
1 garlic clove
2 ounces light cream cheese
3 tablespoons freshly grated Parmesan cheese
1/2 teaspoon grated lemon zest
Pinch of cayenne pepper
Salt and freshly ground black pepper to taste
18 thin slices prosciutto (about 7 ounces)

Heat the olive oil in a small skillet over medium heat. Add the almonds and sauté for 5 minutes or until golden brown. Remove to a plate and let cool. Pulse the artichoke hearts, garlic and almonds in a food processor until finely chopped. Add the cream cheese, Parmesan cheese, lemon zest, cayenne pepper, salt and black pepper and process to a paste. Add additional olive oil if the mixture seems too thick. Lay 3 prosciutto slices on a work surface with the edges slightly overlapping. Spoon 2 tablespoons of the artichoke mixture over the narrow end and roll up. Repeat to use the remaining prosciutto and artichoke mixture. Cut the rolls into halves or quarters. Chill, covered, until ready to serve. The artichoke filling also makes a wonderful dip for crudités.

Serves 12

Crescent Roll Mushroom Tarts

2 tablespoons butter
4 (8-ounce) packages mushrooms, finely chopped
2 tablespoons butter
2 cups finely chopped sweet onions
3 tablespoons chopped fresh chives
1^1/$_2$ ounces cream cheese, cut into small pieces
2 tablespoons all-purpose flour
^{1}/$_2$ cup (2 ounces) grated Parmesan cheese
^{1}/$_2$ teaspoon salt
1 to 2 tablespoons milk (optional)
3 (8-count) cans refrigerator crescent rolls

Melt 2 tablespoons butter in a skillet over medium heat. Add the mushrooms and sauté until tender and most of the liquid has evaporated. Remove the mushrooms with a slotted spoon to a large saucepan. Pour the mushroom liquid into a small bowl and let cool. Add 2 tablespoons butter to the skillet and melt over medium heat. Add the onions and sauté until very tender. Add the chives and sauté for 1 minute. Remove from the heat and add the cream cheese. Stir until the cream cheese is melted. Whisk the flour into the mushroom liquid. Add to the mushrooms in the saucepan and mix gently. Add the Parmesan cheese and salt. Stir in the onion mixture. Cook over low heat for 2 minutes or until the mixture begins to thicken, stirring gently. Stir in the milk if the mixture seems too thick. Remove from the heat and let cool.

Separate 1 can of crescent rolls into 8 pieces on a work surface. Cut each piece in half. Fit each piece of dough into a miniature muffin cup coated with nonstick cooking spray. Spoon 1 heaping teaspoon of the mushroom mixture into each prepared cup. Bake at 375 degrees for 16 minutes or until the edges are puffed and light brown. Cool in the pan for 3 minutes. Remove the tarts to a wire rack or plate. Repeat with the remaining crescent dough and mushroom mixture.

Serve hot or let cool completely and chill in an airtight container. Warm the tarts on a baking sheet at 350 degrees for 10 minutes. The mushroom filling can be made up to two days ahead. Chill, covered, until ready to use.

Serves 24

Blue Cheese Ginger Pennies

1 1/2 cups all-purpose flour
3/4 teaspoon ground ginger
3/4 teaspoon ground cinnamon
1/2 teaspoon ground cloves
1/2 teaspoon baking soda
1/4 teaspoon salt
3/4 cup (1 1/2 sticks) unsalted butter, softened
1 cup packed brown sugar
1 egg
1/4 cup unsulfured molasses
4 ounces crumbled blue cheese
1/4 cup finely chopped crystallized ginger (optional)

Sift the flour, ground ginger, cinnamon, cloves, baking soda and salt together Beat the
butter, brown sugar, egg and molasses in a bowl until light and fluffy. Add the dry
ingredients and mix well. Spoon the mixture into a sealable plastic freezer bag. Cut
off a small corner of the bag. Pipe 1/8-teaspoon dots of dough, 1 inch apart, onto a
nonstick baking sheet. Bake at 325 degrees for 5 minutes or until golden brown. Cool
on the baking sheet for 3 minutes. Remove to a wire rack to cool completely. Store in
an airtight container at room temperature or freeze. Top each wafer with a small piece
of blue cheese and small piece of crystallized ginger when ready to serve. These are
wonderful served with Cranberry Mascarpone Spread (page 38), Pumpkin Dip
(page 39) or as a dessert cookie.

Serves 60

Cheese Puffs

1/2 small onion, finely chopped
1/2 cup mayonnaise
3 tablespoons freshly grated Parmigiano-Reggiano cheese
2 tablespoons finely chopped fresh parsley
Salt and pepper to taste
8 slices thin white bread, crusts removed
Freshly grated Parmigiano-Reggiano cheese

Combine the onion, mayonnaise, 3 tablespoons cheese, the parsley, salt and pepper in a bowl and mix well. Cut 32 rounds from the bread using a 1-inch biscuit cutter. Arrange the rounds on a baking sheet. Bake at 350 degrees for 8 to 10 minutes or until golden brown; do not turn during baking. Spread about 1 teaspoon of the onion mixture over each toasted bread round. Sprinkle with cheese. Broil for 1 to 2 minutes or until golden brown. Serve immediately.

Serves 16

Cheesy Dates

1/2 cup (1 stick) butter, softened
3 ounces cream cheese, softened
1 cup all-purpose flour
1/8 teaspoon salt
1 cup chopped dates
1/4 cup sugar
1/4 cup water
1/2 cup chopped walnuts
1 teaspoon grated orange zest
1/2 cup confectioners' sugar

Beat the butter and cream cheese in a bowl with an electric mixer until light and fluffy. Beat in the flour and salt. Shape the dough into a ball and wrap in waxed paper. Chill for 1 hour. Combine the dates, sugar and water in a saucepan. Cook over medium heat for 3 to 5 minutes or until thickened, stirring frequently. Remove from the heat and stir in the walnuts and orange zest. Let cool to room temperature. Roll out half the dough on a lightly floured work surface to 1/8-inch thickness. Cut into rounds with a 2¹/²-inch biscuit cutter. Place the rounds on a lightly greased baking sheet. Repeat with the remaining dough. Spoon 1/2 teaspoon of the date mixture onto the center of each round. Fold the dough over the filling, pressing the edges of the dough with a fork to seal. Bake at 375 degrees for 15 minutes or until light brown. Remove the pastries to a wire rack to cool. Dust with the confectioners' sugar when cool.

Serves 18

Cheddar Rye Rounds

3 cups (12 ounces) shredded sharp Cheddar cheese
1 (3-ounce) can chopped black olives
1 cup finely chopped green onions
1/2 cup chopped fresh or canned jalapeño chiles
1 cup mayonnaise
2/3 cup crumbled crisp-cooked bacon (12 ounces uncooked)
1 package party rye bread rounds or squares

Combine the cheese, olives, green onions, jalapeños, mayonnaise and bacon in a bowl and mix well. Spread equal portions on the bread rounds and place on a baking sheet. Bake at 300 degrees for 15 to 20 minutes, watching carefully so that the cheese doesn't burn. These can be frozen before baking. Place between layers of waxed paper in an airtight container. Adjust the baking time if frozen when baked.

Serves 24

Spinach Crostini

1 (10-ounce) package frozen chopped spinach,
    thawed, drained and squeezed dry
2 plum tomatoes, diced
1 garlic clove, minced, or to taste
1/2 cup (2 ounces) crumbled feta cheese
1/4 cup mayonnaise
1/4 cup sour cream
1/4 teaspoon pepper
1/8 teaspoon salt, or taste
1 (16-ounce) baguette or French bread loaf,
    cut into 1/2-inch slices

Combine the spinach, tomatoes, garlic, cheese, mayonnaise, sour cream, pepper and salt in a bowl and mix well. Spread equal portions over the bread slices and place on a baking sheet. Bake at 350 degrees for 18 minutes or until golden brown.

Serves 18

Savory Spinach Appetizer Cheesecake

1 (12-ounce) package frozen spinach soufflé
1 cup (4 ounces) grated Parmesan cheese
16 ounces chive and onion cream cheese, softened
6 ounces goat cheese, softened
3 eggs, lightly beaten
1 teaspoon pepper
1/2 teaspoon oregano
1/2 teaspoon basil
1/2 teaspoon thyme
2 garlic cloves, crushed
1/4 cup Italian-style bread crumbs

Microwave the spinach soufflé on Medium for 6 to 7 minutes to thaw. Combine the spinach soufflé, Parmesan cheese, cream cheese, goat cheese, eggs, pepper, oregano, basil, thyme and garlic in a bowl and mix well. Sprinkle the bread crumbs over the bottom of a 9-inch springform pan coated with nonstick cooking spray. Spoon the spinach mixture into the prepared pan. Bake at 325 degrees for 50 to 55 minutes or just until set. Remove to a wire rack to cool completely. Chill, covered, for 8 hours.

Loosen from the side of the pan with a sharp knife and remove the side. Garnish with sour cream, toasted pine nuts and grated Parmesan cheese and serve with crackers. The baked cheesecake can be cut into small wedges and frozen. It can also be made in three 4 1/2-inch springform pans and baked for 35 to 40 minutes.

Serves 36

Smoked Salmon Gâteau

2 tablespoons panko
  (Japanese bread crumbs)
2 tablespoons freshly grated
  Parmesan cheese
3 tablespoons butter
1 cup chopped onion
1 cup chopped red bell pepper
1 garlic clove, crushed
8 to 10 ounces smoked salmon
  trimmings, chopped
1/2 cup (2 ounces) grated
  Gruyère cheese

3 tablespoons freshly grated
  Parmesan cheese
1/2 teaspoon salt, or to taste
1/8 teaspoon freshly ground
  white pepper
1 tablespoon lemon juice
1/8 teaspoon hot red pepper sauce
20 ounces light cream cheese, softened
4 eggs
1/3 cup heavy cream or fat-free
  half-and-half

Mix the panko and 2 tablespoons Parmesan cheese together. Sprinkle into a buttered 8-inch springform pan. Tilt the pan to evenly coat with the panko mixture. Wrap foil around the bottom and 2 inches up the side of the pan. Melt the butter in a skillet. Add the onion, bell pepper and garlic and sauté for 5 minutes or until the vegetables are tender. Remove from the heat and let cool. Fold in the salmon, Gruyère cheese, 3 tablespoons Parmesan cheese, the salt, pepper, lemon juice and hot sauce. Beat the cream cheese, eggs and cream in a large bowl with an electric mixer until smooth. Fold in the salmon mixture. Pour into the prepared pan. Place the springform pan in a larger baking pan. Add enough boiling water to the larger pan to come 2 inches up the side of the springform pan. Bake at 300 degrees for 1 hour or until set. Turn off the oven. Remove the springform pan carefully from the water and return it to the oven. Leave in the oven for 1 hour. Remove to a wire rack and let cool for 2 hours.

Loosen from the side of the pan with a sharp knife and remove the side. Garnish with chopped fresh parsley pressed into the sides of the cheesecake or chopped green onions arranged around the bottom edge. Serve with water crackers, whole grain wheat crackers or pumpernickel bread. This can be made ahead. Chill, covered, until ready to serve. Let stand at room temperature for 1 hour before serving. The recipe may be halved and baked in a 4 1/2-inch springform pan or make three-quarters of the recipe and bake in a 6-inch springform pan. Adjust baking time for smaller pans.

Serves 30

Cheddar and Cream Cheese Ball

16 ounces extra sharp Cheddar cheese
8 ounces cream cheese, softened
8 ounces chive and onion cream cheese, softened
2 teaspoons paprika
1/2 teaspoon pepper, or to taste
Red and green apple slices

Pulse the Cheddar cheese in a food processor until finely chopped. Add the cream cheese, chive and onion cream cheese, paprika and pepper and process well. Chill, covered, for 4 hours or until firm. Shape the mixture into a ball and place on a serving plate. Surround with apple slices. For fall entertaining, form the cheese mixture into a pumpkin shape, making vertical grooves with your fingers. Shape a broccoli stalk to resemble the stem and insert in the top.

Serves 36

Stuffed Brie

1 (6-inch) wheel ripe Brie cheese
1 (5-ounce) can chunk white chicken breast, drained, or
    5 ounces grilled chicken
1/4 cup prepared pesto
3 tablespoons toasted finely chopped pecans
1 to 2 teaspoons honey

Cut the cheese in half crosswise. Place the bottom half, cut side up, on a microwave-safe plate. Remove the rind from the top half of the cheese. Flake or shred the chicken into a bowl. Add the pesto and mix well. Spread over the bottom half of the cheese. Top with the other cheese half. Sprinkle with the pecans and drizzle with the honey. Microwave on Medium for 1 1/2 to 2 minutes or until the cheese is warm or bake at 350 degrees for 15 to 20 minutes. Serve hot with crackers or toast rounds.

Serves 12

♩ Unlike hard cheeses, when soft cheeses such as Brie show signs of mold they should be discarded immediately.

Pesto Pie

5 to 6 ounces goat cheese, softened
8 ounces cream cheese, softened
1 teaspoon lemon juice
1 cup torn fresh spinach
1 cup chopped fresh basil
2 or 3 garlic cloves
3 tablespoons olive oil
Salt and pepper to taste
1 cup boiling water
1 1/2 ounces sun-dried tomatoes, chopped
1/2 cup finely chopped pecans

Beat the goat cheese, cream cheese and lemon juice in a bowl until smooth. Combine the spinach, basil, garlic, olive oil, salt and pepper in a blender and process well. Pour the boiling water over sun-dried tomatoes in a bowl. Let stand until the tomatoes soften. Drain and squeeze dry. Spread half the cream cheese mixture over the bottom of a 6-inch cereal bowl lined with plastic wrap. Top with the sun-dried tomatoes. Spread the spinach mixture over the sun-dried tomatoes. Top with the remaining cream cheese mixture and sprinkle with the pecans. Cover with plastic wrap and chill for 24 hours. Unmold onto a serving plate and remove the plastic wrap. Smooth the surface with a knife dipped in hot water. Garnish with fresh basil sprigs. Serve with bagel chips or crackers.

Serves 20

Walnut Cheese Pie

2 tablespoons sour cream
8 ounces cream cheese, softened
3/4 cup chopped walnuts or pecans
16 ounces cream cheese, softened
4 ounces Gruyère cheese, grated
4 ounces crumbled blue cheese
4 ounces Brie cheese, softened

Combine the sour cream and 8 ounces cream cheese in a bowl and mix well. Spread over the bottom of a springform pan lined with waxed paper. Sprinkle with the walnuts. Combine 16 ounces cream cheese, the Gruyère cheese, blue cheese and Brie cheese in a bowl and mix well. Spread over the cream cheese layer in the pan. Chill, covered, for 2 days. Loosen from the side of the pan with a sharp knife and remove the side. Invert onto a serving plate and immediately remove the waxed paper. Sprinkle with a mixture of chopped fresh parsley and paprika. Serve with crackers or bread slices.

Serves 24

♪ Hard and semi-firm cheeses may be frozen. Freezing cheese will change its texture, and it is best used for baking.

Country Ham Spread

8 ounces country-cured ham
8 ounces Virginia-baked ham
4 ounces cream cheese, softened
Juice of 1 lemon
Worcestershire sauce to taste
Pepper to taste

Pulse the country-cured ham and Virginia-baked ham in a food processor until finely chopped but not mushy. Add the cream cheese, lemon juice, Worcestershire sauce and pepper and process well. Remove to a serving bowl. Chill, covered, overnight. Serve at room temperature with Angel Biscuits (page 64).

Serves 36

Creamy Smoked Trout Spread

1/3 cup light mayonnaise
1/3 cup light sour cream
4 1/2 teaspoons lemon juice
1/2 teaspoon Dijon mustard
1/4 cup chopped fresh chives or green onions
10 ounces skinless smoked trout fillets, coarsely chopped
1 Granny Smith apple, cored and chopped (optional)
Salt and pepper to taste

Combine the mayonnaise, sour cream, lemon juice, Dijon mustard and chives in a bowl and mix well. Add the trout, apple, salt and pepper and toss gently. Chill, covered, for up to 24 hours. Smoked salmon may be used instead of smoked trout and substitute 1 tablespoon capers for the apple.

Serves 12

Shrimp Cocktail Spread

16 ounces cream cheese, softened
1/2 cup ketchup
2 tablespoons finely chopped onion
1 tablespoon Worcestershire sauce
1 teaspoon lemon juice
1/2 teaspoon salt

1/2 teaspoon pepper
1/2 teaspoon hot red pepper sauce
1 pound peeled cooked shrimp,
    chopped
Horseradish (optional)
Paprika

Combine the cream cheese, ketchup, onion, Worcestershire sauce, lemon juice, salt, pepper, hot sauce, shrimp and horseradish in a bowl and mix well. Spoon into a serving dish and sprinkle with paprika. Chill, covered, overnight. Serve on butter crackers, corn chips or celery.

Serves 24

Black Olive Tapenade

Grated zest of 1/2 lemon
1 cup pitted kalamata olives
    (about 5 ounces)
1/2 teaspoon finely chopped fresh
    rosemary
1 small garlic clove, crushed

1 tablespoon extra-virgin olive oil
1 teaspoon (or more) fresh lemon juice
Salt and freshly ground pepper to taste
Thinly sliced roasted red bell pepper
Capers

Pulse the lemon zest, olives, rosemary and garlic in a food processor until coarsely chopped. Add the olive oil gradually, pulsing to a thick paste. Remove to a bowl. Stir in the lemon juice, salt and pepper. Top with roasted bell pepper strips and capers. Serve with toast points.

Serves 6

Sun-Dried Tomato Cheese Spread

8 ounces cream cheese, softened
1/2 cup (1 stick) unsalted butter, softened
1/2 cup (2 ounces) grated Parmesan cheese
1/4 cup oil-pack sun-dried tomatoes, drained

2 tablespoons oil from the sun-dried tomatoes
1 tablespoon chopped fresh basil, or 1 teaspoon dried basil

Combine the cream cheese, butter, Parmesan cheese, sun-dried tomatoes, sun-dried tomato oil and basil in a food processor. Pulse to mix well. Remove to a serving bowl or crock. Chill, covered, until ready to serve. Serve at room temperature with pita wedges or Toasted Flat Bread (page 64).

Serves 16

Feta Cheese Dip

8 ounces crumbled feta cheese
1/2 cup mayonnaise or light mayonnaise
1/2 cup fat-free plain yogurt
1 garlic clove, crushed
1 tablespoon (or more) finely chopped pepperoncini

1 tablespoon lemon juice
4 1/2 teaspoons chopped fresh oregano, or 3/4 teaspoon dried oregano
Several dashes of hot red pepper sauce
Salt and pepper to taste

Combine the cheese, mayonnaise, yogurt, garlic, pepperoncini, lemon juice, oregano, hot sauce, salt and pepper in a food processor. Process for 1 minute or until well mixed but still chunky. Remove to a serving bowl and garnish with kalamata olives. Serve with pita wedges, red bell pepper strips, cucumber slices and carrot sticks. It can also be used as a spread on ham or vegetable sandwiches or thinned with buttermilk and used as a salad dressing.

Serves 16

Lemon Basil Dip

3/4 cup mayonnaise
3/4 cup low-fat plain yogurt
1/3 cup chopped fresh basil
1/2 teaspoon grated lemon zest
1 tablespoon fresh lemon juice
1/8 teaspoon cayenne pepper
1 1/4 pounds fresh peeled shrimp
1 pound sugar snap peas

Combine the mayonnaise, yogurt, basil, lemon zest, lemon juice and cayenne pepper in a bowl and mix well. Chill, covered, for up to 24 hours. Cook the shrimp in a saucepan of boiling seasoned water until the shrimp turn pink. Drain and place in a bowl. Chill, covered, until cold. Cook the sugar snap peas in a saucepan of boiling salted water for 45 seconds. Drain and plunge into ice water until cold. Drain and pat dry. Spoon the dip into a serving bowl and place on a platter. Surround with the shrimp and sugar snap peas. For a thicker dip, drain the yogurt in a sieve before adding. This dip is also good on poached, baked or grilled salmon.

Serves 24

Hot Mexican-Style Spinach Dip

1 tablespoon vegetable oil
1 onion, chopped
2 tomatoes, seeded and chopped
2 tablespoons seeded chopped canned jalapeño chile
1 (10-ounce) package frozen chopped spinach, thawed and well drained
3/4 cup half-and-half or milk
2 cups (8 ounces) shredded Monterey Jack cheese
8 ounces low-fat cream cheese, cut into 1/2-inch cubes
1 tablespoon red wine vinegar
1/4 teaspoon salt
1/4 teaspoon pepper
2 (2-ounce) cans sliced black olives, drained (optional)

Heat the oil in a skillet over medium-high heat. Add the onion and sauté for 4 minutes or until tender. Add the tomatoes and jalapeño and sauté for 2 minutes longer. Remove to a large bowl. Add the spinach, half-and-half, Monterey Jack cheese, cream cheese, vinegar, salt, pepper and olives and mix well. Spoon into a greased 2-quart baking dish. Bake at 400 degrees for 35 minutes or until golden brown and bubbly. Serve warm with tortilla chips.

Serves 48

Gazpacho Dip

1 (28-ounce) can whole tomatoes, drained and juice reserved
1 (8-ounce) can tomato sauce
2 tablespoons red wine vinegar
1 tablespoon olive oil
1 (4-ounce) can diced green chiles
1 garlic clove, crushed
4 ounces mushrooms, chopped
1 bunch green onions, thinly sliced
1/4 teaspoon salt
1/4 teaspoon garlic salt
Freshly ground pepper to taste

Mash the tomatoes with your fingers in a nonreactive bowl. Add the tomato sauce, vinegar, olive oil, green chiles, garlic, mushrooms, green onions, salt, garlic salt and pepper and mix well. Stir in some of the reserved tomato juice if the mixture seems too thick. Chill, covered, overnight. Serve with tortilla chips, cucumber slices and celery. This is a very healthy appetizer. It is also delicious tossed with hot cooked pasta.

Serves 32

Cranberry Mascarpone Spread

8 ounces mascarpone cheese, softened
1 teaspoon grated orange zest
1 tablespoon Grand Marnier or orange juice
Pinch of salt
1/3 cup sweetened dried cranberries or dried cherries, chopped
1 tablespoon milk or Grand Marnier (optional)

Combine the cheese, orange zest, 1 tablespoon Grand Marnier and the salt in a bowl. Beat with an electric mixer at medium speed until smooth. Stir in the dried cranberries. Stir in 1 tablespoon milk, if needed to make a spreadable consistency. Chill, covered, until cold. Bring to room temperature before serving. Serve with gingersnap cookies, Pirouline cookies or Blue Cheese Ginger Pennies (page 21).

Serves 12

♪ Mascarpone is a buttery, rich cream cheese with 65 percent to 75 percent milk fat. Its slightly sweet flavor is delicious served with fruit.

Apple Brickle Dip

8 ounces cream cheese, softened
1/2 cup packed brown sugar
1/4 cup granulated sugar
1 teaspoon vanilla extract
1 (8-ounce) package almond brickle chips or toffee chips
4 apples, cored and sliced

Beat the cream cheese, brown sugar, granulated sugar and vanilla in a bowl with an electric mixer until smooth. Fold in the almond brickle chips. Chill, covered, until cold. Bring to room temperature before serving. Serve with the apple slices.

Serves 12

Pumpkin Dip

16 ounces light whipped cream cheese, softened
1 (16-ounce) package confectioners' sugar, sifted
1 (16-ounce) can pumpkin
2 teaspoons ground cinnamon
1/2 teaspoon nutmeg

Beat the cream cheese, confectioners' sugar, pumpkin, cinnamon and nutmeg in a bowl with an electric mixer until smooth. Spoon into a serving bowl. Serve with apples slices or Blue Cheese Ginger Pennies (page 21).

Serves 32

 To prevent apple slices from turning brown, soak in salt water. Rinse and pat dry before serving.

Strawberry Salsa

1 1/2 cups diced fresh strawberries
1/2 cup diced fresh mango or papaya
1/2 jalapeño chile, seeded and finely chopped
2 tablespoons chopped fresh cilantro
1 teaspoon lime juice
Pinch of sugar
Salt to taste

Combine the strawberries, mango, jalapeño, cilantro, lime juice, sugar and salt in a bowl and toss well. Let stand for 10 minutes. Serve with tortilla chips.

Serves 16

Salted Butter Pecans

5 tablespoons butter
3 cups pecan halves
Salt to taste

Melt the butter in a saucepan. Add the pecans and toss well to coat. Spread the pecans over the bottom of a 10×15-inch baking pan. Sprinkle heavily with salt. Bake at 250 degrees for 1 hour, stirring every 15 minutes. Season with additional salt after 45 minutes of baking, if desired. Remove to a wire rack and let cool completely. Store in an airtight container. Serve as an appetizer or toss with salad greens and fresh fruit or dried fruit in a salad.

Serves 24

Spiced Nuts

1 egg white
2 tablespoons cold water
1/2 cup sugar
1/2 teaspoon salt
1/4 teaspoon ground cinnamon
1/4 teaspoon ground allspice
1/4 teaspoon ground cloves
4 cups pecan halves

Combine the egg white, water, sugar, salt, cinnamon, allspice and cloves in a large bowl and mix well. Let stand for 15 minutes. Add the pecans and toss well to coat. Spread the pecans over 2 greased baking sheets. Bake at 200 degrees for 1 hour. Remove to a wire rack and break apart the pecans. Let cool completely.

Serves 32

♪ When buying pecans, look for a light brown color for the freshest pecans.

Iced Almond Latte

1 cup finely ground espresso coffee beans
1¹/2 cups cold water
1 cup finely ground espresso coffee beans
1¹/2 cups cold water
3 tablespoons brown sugar
1¹/2 cups milk
5 teaspoons almond syrup
Whipped cream
1 teaspoon finely ground espresso coffee beans

Place 1 cup ground espresso in the filter basket of a coffee maker and pour 1¹/2 cups water into the reservoir. Brew the coffee. Pour the brewed coffee into a bowl. Repeat with 1 cup ground espresso and 1¹/2 cups water. Add the brewed coffee to the bowl. Add the brown sugar and stir until the sugar is dissolved. Stir in the milk and almond syrup. Chill, covered, 2 hours to overnight. Fill 6 glasses with ice cubes. Divide the coffee mixture among the glasses. Top with whipped cream and sprinkle with 1 teaspoon ground espresso.

Serves 6

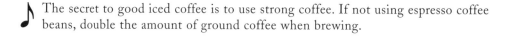 The secret to good iced coffee is to use strong coffee. If not using espresso coffee beans, double the amount of ground coffee when brewing.

42

Iced Irish Coffee Nog

1 quart eggnog
1¹/4 cups strong brewed coffee, chilled
2/3 cup Irish cream liqueur
1/2 cup brandy
1/2 cup sugar

Combine the eggnog, coffee, Irish cream liqueur, brandy and sugar in a large pitcher. Stir until the sugar is dissolved. Chill, covered, until cold. Store any leftovers in the refrigerator.

Serves 10 to 12

Midnight Mozart

4¹/2 teaspoons Kahlúa
4¹/2 teaspoons Mozart liqueur
Brewed hot coffee
Heavy cream or whipped cream (optional)

Pour the Kahlúa and Mozart liqueur into a coffee cup. Add the coffee and cream or use chilled brewed coffee and a scoop of vanilla ice cream instead of cream for an iced version.

Serves 1

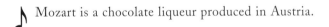 Mozart is a chocolate liqueur produced in Austria.

Minted Vodka Lemonade

1 cup packed fresh mint, chopped
1/3 cup sugar
1 cup fresh lemon juice
1 1/2 cups vodka

Mix the mint and sugar in a bowl. Add the lemon juice and vodka and stir well. Chill, covered, for 1 to 2 hours. Strain into a pitcher. Serve over glasses of crushed ice and garnish each glass with a mint sprig.

Serves 6

Champagne Punch

2 cups lemon juice
3 cups sugar
1 fresh pineapple, peeled, cored and cubed
1 cup sugar
6 cups ice water
1 (750-milliliter) bottle sauterne or Rhine wine, chilled
1 quart fresh strawberries
1 tablespoon sugar
2 (750-milliliter) bottles Champagne, chilled

Combine the lemon juice and 3 cups sugar in a bowl. Stir until the sugar is dissolved. Dredge the pineapple in 1 cup sugar. Place the pineapple in a chilled punch bowl. Add the lemon juice mixture. Stir in the water and sauterne. Add a block of ice or ice mold. Toss the strawberries with 1 tablespoon sugar in a bowl Add to the punch. Add the champagne and stir gently. Serve immediately.

Serves 24

Firecracker Punch

    4 cups cranberry juice cocktail
    1 1/2 cups sugar
    4 cups pineapple juice
    1 tablespoon almond extract
    2 quarts ginger ale, chilled

Combine the cranberry juice cocktail, sugar, pineapple juice and almond extract in a bowl. Stir until the sugar is dissolved. Chill, covered, until cold. Pour into a punch bowl or very large pitcher. Add the ginger ale and stir gently.

Serves 16

Bourbon Slush

    2 cups sugar
    6 cups water
    2 cups brewed tea
    1 (12-ounce) can frozen lemonade concentrate, thawed
    1 (6-ounce) can frozen orange juice concentrate, thawed
    1 1/2 cups bourbon

Combine the sugar, water, tea, lemonade concentrate, orange juice concentrate and bourbon in a large sealable plastic freezer container. Stir until the sugar is dissolved. Freeze until firm. Remove from the freezer and let stand for 15 minutes. Stir until slushy and spoon into glasses.

Serves 12

Cranberry Tea

1 cup sugar
2 cups water
2 cinnamon sticks
15 whole cloves

5 tea bags
8 cups apple juice
4 cups cranberry juice cocktail
Brandy (optional)

Combine the sugar, water, cinnamon sticks and cloves in a saucepan. Bring to a boil and boil for 5 minutes, stirring occasionally. Remove from the heat and add the tea bags. Let steep for 10 minutes. Remove the tea bags. Stir in the apple juice and cranberry juice cocktail. Chill until ready to serve. Heat to a gentle simmer and keep warm. Pour into mugs and add a splash of brandy.

Serves 12 to 14

Pineapple-Orange Tea

1 gallon water
8 tea bags
2½ cups sugar
2 cups water

2 tablespoons whole cloves
1 (46-ounce) can pineapple juice
1 (46-ounce) can orange juice

Bring 1 gallon water to a boil in a large saucepan. Add the tea bags and remove from the heat. Let steep for 3 minutes. Remove and discard the tea bags. Combine the sugar and 2 cups water in a saucepan. Bring to a boil, stirring occasionally. Add the cloves and boil for 10 minutes, stirring frequently until syrupy. Add to the tea. Stir in the pineapple juice and orange juice. Strain to remove the cloves. Chill, covered, for 4 hours to overnight. Serve hot or cold.

Serves 32

Preludes
Breakfast, Brunch & Breads

Fund-Raising

Since 1984, the Guild has raised well over $1 million in support of the Greensboro Symphony Orchestra and its education programs, which reach more than 50,000 people annually in Greensboro and the surrounding area. Many fund-raisers have provided funding throughout the years for the Endowment and various Guild- and Orchestra-sponsored music education programs. Major fund-raisers such as the Presentation Ball, Homes Tour, Golf Classic, and Super Sale have been staples of the Guild's fund-raising efforts for many years.

Cotten Moring's painting of a welcoming front door was selected as the cover image of the 2005 Homes Tour booklet. A native of Bethel, North Carolina, Cotten served as Chair of the Homes Tour in her first year as a member of the Guild. She is also an active Sustainer member of the Junior League.

French Toast Soufflé

10 cups 1-inch firm white bread cubes (about 16 slices bread)
8 ounces reduced-fat cream cheese, softened
8 eggs
1$^{1}/_{2}$ cups 2% milk
$^{2}/_{3}$ cup half-and-half or fat-free half-and-half
$^{1}/_{2}$ cup maple syrup
$^{1}/_{2}$ teaspoon vanilla extract
2 tablespoons confectioners' sugar

Spread the bread cubes over the bottom of a 9×13-inch baking dish coated with nonstick cooking spray. Beat the cream cheese in a bowl until smooth. Add the eggs, one at a time, beating well after each addition. Beat in the milk, half-and-half, maple syrup and vanilla. Pour evenly over the bread cubes. Chill, covered, overnight. Let stand at room temperature for 30 minutes before baking. Bake at 375 degrees for 50 minutes or until set. Sprinkle with the confectioners' sugar. Serve with maple syrup.

Serves 12

Baked French Toast with Apples

1/2 cup (1 stick) butter
1 cup packed brown sugar
2 tablespoons dark corn syrup
4 Granny Smith apples, peeled, cored and sliced
1 loaf French or Italian bread, cut into 1/2- to 1-inch slices
6 eggs
1 1/2 cups milk
1 teaspoon vanilla extract
Pinch of nutmeg
Ground cinnamon
Butter (optional)

Combine 1/2 cup butter, the brown sugar and corn syrup in a saucepan. Bring to a
boil, stirring occasionally. Pour evenly over the bottom of a 9×13-inch baking dish. Top
with the apple slices in a single layer. Arrange the bread slices over the apples. Combine
the eggs, milk, vanilla and nutmeg in a bowl and mix well. Pour evenly over the bread.
Sprinkle with cinnamon. Chill, covered, overnight. Bake at 350 degrees for 1 hour,
dotting with butter halfway through baking.

Serves 8

Sausage and Grits Casserole

3/4 cup grits
3 cups water
4 cups (16 ounces) shredded Cheddar cheese
4 eggs
1 cup milk
1/4 teaspoon garlic powder
1 1/2 pounds bulk pork sausage, cooked, drained and crumbled
1/3 cup chopped green onions (optional)

Cook the grits in the water in a large saucepan according to the package directions. Remove from the heat and stir in the cheese. Whisk the eggs, milk and garlic powder in a bowl. Add to the grits and mix well. Stir in the sausage. Pour into a greased 9×13-inch baking dish. Bake at 350 degrees for 50 minutes. Top with the green onions. You may make this one day ahead. Chill, covered, overnight. Adjust the baking time. You may add additional green onions before baking, if desired.

Serves 8 to 10

Sausage and Cheese Brunch Tarts

1¹/₄ cups biscuit mix
¹/₄ cup (¹/₂ stick) butter, softened
2 tablespoons boiling water
8 ounces bulk pork sausage, cooked,
  crumbled and drained
1 egg

¹/₂ cup half-and-half
2 tablespoons thinly sliced
  green onions
¹/₄ teaspoon salt
¹/₂ cup (2 ounces) shredded
  Swiss cheese

Combine the baking mix and butter in a bowl and stir well. Add the boiling water and stir vigorously until a stiff dough forms. Press 1 level tablespoon of dough over the bottom and up the side of each of 12 well-greased muffin cups. Divide the sausage evenly among the prepared muffin cups. Whisk the egg and half-and-half in a bowl. Stir in the green onions and salt. Spoon about 1 tablespoon of the egg mixture over the sausage in each muffin cup. Sprinkle evenly with the cheese. Bake at 375 degrees for 25 minutes or until the edges are golden brown and the centers are set. Serve immediately or let cool and chill, covered, until ready to serve. Reheat before serving.

Serves 12

Sausage Wellington

1 pound bulk pork sausage
8 ounces cream cheese, softened
1 (8-count) can refrigerator
  crescent rolls

1 egg white, lightly beaten
1 tablespoon sesame seeds

Brown the sausage in a skillet, stirring until crumbly; drain. Add the cream cheese and cook until creamy, stirring frequently. Remove from the heat. Unroll the crescent dough on a work surface to form 4 long rectangles. Press the seams to seal. Spread the sausage mixture lengthwise down the center of each rectangle. Fold the sides over the center to form logs and press the ends to seal. Brush with the egg white and sprinkle with the sesame seeds. Place on a nonstick baking sheet. Bake at 350 degrees for 20 to 30 minutes or until golden brown.

Serves 4

Ham and Cheese Quiche with Hash Brown Crust

3 cups grated peeled potatoes or frozen hash
   brown potatoes, thawed and patted dry
1 tablespoon butter, melted
1 teaspoon Creole seasoning
1/8 teaspoon salt
1/4 cup (1 ounce) freshly grated Parmesan cheese
4 eggs
11/2 cups half-and-half
1/4 teaspoon pepper
1/2 teaspoon salt
1 cup (4 ounces) shredded Swiss cheese
1/2 cup (2 ounces) shredded Cheddar cheese
4 ounces baked ham, chopped

Combine the potatoes, melted butter, Creole seasoning and 1/8 teaspoon salt in a bowl
and toss well. Add the Parmesan cheese and toss well. Press the potato mixture over
the bottom and up the side of a lightly greased 9-inch pie plate. Bake at 425 degrees for
25 minutes or until golden brown. Remove to a wire rack to cool. Whisk the eggs in a
bowl. Whisk in the half-and-half, pepper and 1/2 teaspoon salt. Stir in the Swiss cheese,
Cheddar cheese and ham. Pour into the baked crust. Bake at 350 degrees for 30 minutes
or until golden brown and the center is almost set. Remove to a wire rack and let cool
20 minutes before serving.

Serves 6 to 8

Bacon Quiche

2 tablespoons butter
2 onions, chopped
4 egg yolks
8 ounces cream cheese, softened
1 cup sliced mushrooms
1 teaspoon Tabasco sauce or Texas Pete sauce
1 teaspoon salt
1/4 teaspoon pepper
4 egg whites
8 slices bacon, crisp-cooked and crumbled
2 unbaked (9-inch) pie shells

Melt the butter in a skillet. Add the onions and sauté until tender. Mix the onions, egg yolks, cream cheese, mushrooms, Tabasco sauce, salt and pepper in a food processor or in a bowl with an electric mixer. Beat the egg whites in a bowl with an electric mixer until stiff. Fold into the cream cheese mixture. Fold in the bacon. Pour into the pie shells. Bake at 400 degrees for 35 minutes or until a knife inserted in the center comes out clean.

Serves 12 to 16

Oven Ham Omelet

8 eggs
1/2 cup sour cream
1/2 teaspoon salt
1 cup (4 ounces) shredded Cheddar cheese or Swiss cheese
1/2 cup chopped ham
2 tablespoons butter, melted

Beat the eggs, sour cream and salt in a bowl. Stir in the cheese and ham. Pour into a greased 1 1/2-quart baking dish. Drizzle with the melted butter. Bake at 350 degrees for 30 to 40 minutes or until set. You may increase the amount of cheese and ham and serve as a main dish.

Serves 4 to 6

Chile Relleno Casserole

4 (7-ounce) cans whole green chiles, drained
16 ounces Monterey Jack cheese, cut into 1/4-inch-thick slices
5 eggs
1 1/4 cups milk
1/4 cup all-purpose flour
1/2 teaspoon salt
Dash of pepper
4 cups (16 ounces) shredded mild Cheddar cheese

Slit the chiles lengthwise on one side and remove the seeds. Stuff each chile with a slice of Monterey Jack cheese. Arrange the stuffed chiles in an ungreased 9×13-inch baking dish. Beat the eggs, milk, flour, salt and pepper in a bowl. Pour evenly over the chiles. Sprinkle with the Cheddar cheese. Bake at 350 degrees for 45 minutes. The chiles may be stuffed one day ahead. Chill, covered, until ready to assemble the casserole.

Serves 8

Caramel Coffee Cake

2 cups all-purpose flour
1 teaspoon baking powder
1/2 teaspoon baking soda
1 cup (2 sticks) butter, softened
1 1/2 cups granulated sugar
2 eggs
1 teaspoon vanilla extract
1 cup sour cream
1/3 cup packed brown sugar
1 1/2 teaspoons ground cinnamon
1 cup pecans, chopped

Mix the flour, baking powder and baking soda together. Beat the butter and granulated sugar in a bowl until light and fluffy. Beat in the eggs and vanilla. Beat in the dry ingredients alternately with the sour cream until creamy. Pour half the batter into a greased and floured 9×13-inch baking pan. Combine the brown sugar, cinnamon and pecans in a bowl and mix well. Sprinkle evenly over the batter in the baking pan. Top with the remaining batter. Bake at 350 degrees for 35 minutes or until the cake tests done. Remove to a wire rack to cool.

Serves 8

Bouchti (Cinnamon Nut Roll)

2 envelopes dry yeast
$1/2$ cup warm water
$11/2$ cups (3 sticks) margarine, melted
   and cooled
$11/2$ cups scalded milk
$1/2$ cup granulated sugar
2 eggs
2 teaspoons salt
7 to 8 cups all-purpose flour

$1/2$ cup (1 stick) butter or
   margarine, melted
4 cups chopped pecans or walnuts
$1/2$ cup granulated sugar
1 teaspoon ground cinnamon
$3/4$ cup confectioners' sugar
1 teaspoon vanilla extract
4 to 6 tablespoons water

Dissolve the yeast in the warm water in a large bowl. Stir in $11/2$ cups cooled melted margarine. Add the milk, $1/2$ cup granulated sugar, the eggs, salt and 6 cups of the flour. Beat with an electric mixer until well mixed. Turn out onto a floured work surface. Add at least 1 cup of the remaining flour and knead for 5 minutes or until stiff. Place in a greased bowl and turn to coat. Cover and let rise in a warm place until doubled in bulk. Punch down the dough and let stand for 10 minutes.

Divide the dough into 4 equal portions. Roll out each portion on a floured work surface to a $1/8$-inch-thick rectangle. Brush with $1/2$ cup melted butter. Combine the pecans, $1/2$ cup granulated sugar and the cinnamon in a bowl and mix well. Sprinkle evenly over the 4 dough rectangles. Roll as for a jelly roll, sealing the edges and ends. Place seam side down on a nonstick baking sheet and cover with a kitchen towel. Let rise in a warm place for 30 minutes. Remove the towel. Bake at 350 degrees for 30 minutes. Remove to a wire rack to cool completely. Mix the confectioners' sugar, vanilla and enough water in a bowl to make a thin icing. Drizzle over the cooled rolls.

These make a great gift for Christmas morning breakfast. You may use prune butter or apple butter instead of the nut mixture for the filling.

Serves 48

Cinnamon Buttermilk Muffins

MUFFINS
1 1/2 cups all-purpose flour
1 1/2 teaspoons baking powder
1/2 teaspoon baking soda
1/2 teaspoon salt
1/2 teaspoon freshly grated nutmeg
7 tablespoons butter, softened
2/3 cup sugar
1 egg
1/2 cup buttermilk
1 1/2 teaspoons vanilla extract

TOPPING
2/3 cup sugar
1 tablespoon ground cinnamon
6 tablespoons butter, melted

For the muffins, mix the flour, baking powder, baking soda, salt and nutmeg together. Beat the butter and sugar in a bowl with an electric mixer at medium speed until light and fluffy. Add the egg and beat well. Stir in the dry ingredients alternately with the buttermilk and vanilla, stirring just until moistened. Coat 9 muffin cups with nonstick cooking spray. Fill prepared cups 3/4 full with the batter. Bake at 350 degrees for 20 to 25 minutes or until a wooden pick inserted in the center comes out clean. Cool in the pan for 5 minutes. Remove to a wire rack to cool slightly.

For the topping, combine the sugar and cinnamon in a small shallow bowl and mix well. Pour the melted butter into a small bowl. Dip the top of each warm muffin into the melted butter and then into the cinnamon-sugar, coating evenly. Tap the muffin to remove any excess cinnamon-sugar. Set the muffins upright on a wire rack to cool completely.

Serves 9

Polenta- and Herb-Seasoned Muffins

2 cups plus 3 tablespoons all-purpose flour
1 1/4 cups polenta or coarse-ground cornmeal
1/4 cup sugar
1 tablespoon baking powder
1 teaspoon baking soda
1 1/2 teaspoons salt
1/8 teaspoon cayenne pepper
1/2 cup (1 stick) chilled butter, cut into small pieces
1/3 cup olive oil
3 eggs
1 1/3 cups 1% buttermilk
1/4 cup chopped fresh flat-leaf parsley
2 tablespoons finely chopped fresh chives or sweet onion
2 tablespoons finely chopped fresh oregano or basil

Combine the flour, polenta, sugar, baking powder, baking soda, salt and cayenne pepper in a bowl and mix well. Beat in the butter and olive oil with an electric mixer at low speed until crumbly. Add the eggs, buttermilk, parsley, chives and oregano. Beat just until combined. Coat 14 regular muffin cups or 30 miniature muffin cups with nonstick cooking spray. Fill prepared cups to the rim with the batter. Bake at 375 degrees for 20 to 25 minutes for regular muffins or 15 minutes for miniature muffins or until a wooden pick inserted in the center comes out clean. Cool in the pan for 5 minutes. Remove to a wire rack. Serve warm or at room temperature.

Serves 14

 Polenta is a coarse-ground cornmeal. It is an Italian staple that is cooked in water and served soft for breakfast or as a side dish. Soft polenta can also be chilled until firm, and then cut into squares and sautéed or grilled.

Hawaiian Banana Bread

3 cups all-purpose flour
2 cups sugar
1 cup chopped pecans
1 teaspoon baking soda
1 teaspoon salt
1 teaspoon ground cinnamon
3 eggs, beaten
2 cups mashed ripe bananas
1 1/2 cups vegetable oil
1 cup drained crushed pineapple
2 teaspoons vanilla extract

Combine the flour, sugar, pecans, baking soda, salt and cinnamon in a large bowl and
mix well. Combine the eggs, bananas, oil, pineapple and vanilla in a bowl and mix well.
Add to the dry ingredients and stir just until moistened. Pour the batter into two
greased 5×9-inch loaf pans. Bake at 350 degrees for 55 minutes to 1 hour. Cool in the
pans for 10 minutes. Remove to a wire rack to cool completely.

Serves 24

Cranberry Orange Bread

2 cups all-purpose flour
1/2 cup granulated sugar
1/2 cup packed light brown sugar
2 teaspoons baking powder
1/2 teaspoon salt
Grated zest of 1 orange
1 egg
1/4 cup (1/2 stick) butter, melted, or 1/4 cup walnut oil
1/2 cup milk
1/2 cup strained fresh orange juice
11/2 cups fresh cranberries, chopped
1/2 cup pecans or walnuts, chopped

Mix the flour, granulated sugar, brown sugar, baking powder, salt and orange zest together. Whisk the egg, melted butter, milk and orange juice in a large bowl. Add the dry ingredients and stir just until moistened. Fold in the cranberries and pecans just until combined; do not overmix. Spoon the batter into a greased 5×9-inch loaf pan or 10 greased muffin cups. Bake at 375 degrees for 40 minutes for a loaf and 20 to 25 minutes for muffins or until a wooden pick inserted in the center comes out clean. Cool in the pan for 10 minutes. Remove to a wire rack to cool. Serve warm or at room temperature with butter.

Serves 10

 Each 12-ounce package of fresh cranberries contains 3 cups. To have cranberries available year round, freeze fresh cranberries in sealable plastic freezer bags for up to one year. Thaw slightly before using in recipes calling for fresh cranberries.

Lemon Blueberry Bread

1 1/2 cups all-purpose flour
1 teaspoon baking powder
Pinch of salt
6 tablespoons butter, softened
1 cup sugar
2 eggs
1 1/2 cups milk
2 teaspoons grated lemon zest
1 cup fresh blueberries or frozen blueberries
3 tablespoons lemon juice
1/3 cup sugar

Mix the flour, baking powder and salt together. Combine the butter and 1 cup sugar in a bowl. Beat with an electric mixer at medium speed until light and fluffy. Add the eggs one at a time, beating well after each addition. Beat in the dry ingredients alternately with the milk. Stir in the lemon zest. Fold in the blueberries. Pour into a greased 4×8-inch loaf pan. Bake at 350 degrees for 55 minutes or until a wooden pick inserted in the center comes out clean. Remove to a wire rack. Poke small holes in the top of the bread with a fork or wooden pick. Combine the lemon juice and 1/3 cup sugar in a small saucepan. Cook until the sugar is dissolved, stirring constantly. Pour evenly over the top of the warm bread. Let cool in the pan for 30 minutes. Remove to a wire rack to cool completely.

Serves 12

Irish Soda Bread

    3 cups sifted all-purpose flour
    2/3 cup sugar
    1 tablespoon baking powder
    1 teaspoon baking soda
    1 teaspoon salt
    1 1/2 cups raisins
    2 eggs, beaten
    1 3/4 to 2 cups buttermilk
    2 tablespoons shortening, melted

Sift the flour, sugar, baking powder, baking soda and salt into a large bowl. Stir in the raisins. Combine the eggs, buttermilk, and melted shortening in a bowl and mix well. Add to the dry ingredients and stir just until moistened. Pour into a greased loaf pan. Bake at 350 degrees for 1 hour or until the bread tests done. Remove from the pan to a wire rack to cool completely.

Serves 12

Toasted Flat Bread

1 package flat bread or pita bread
3 tablespoons olive oil

Sea salt, poppy seeds, chopped fresh
   rosemary or paprika

Lay the bread on a work surface. Cut out shapes with a cookie cutter and brush the bread lightly with the olive oil. Arrange the bread on a baking sheet. Sprinkle with sea salt, poppy seeds, rosemary or paprika. Bake at 450 degrees for 5 to 7 minutes or until light brown. Flat bread is preferable to pita bread since it is easier to cut and doesn't puff during baking. Chose a flat bread flavor that compliments the dip or spread being served.

Serves 48

Angel Biscuits

1 envelope dry yeast
2 tablespoons warm water
   (105 to 115 degrees)
2 cups buttermilk
5 cups all-purpose flour

1/4 cup sugar
1 tablespoon baking powder
1 teaspoon baking soda
1 teaspoon salt
1 cup shortening

Combine the yeast and the warm water in a bowl. Let stand for 5 minutes or until bubbly. Stir in the buttermilk. Mix the flour, sugar, baking powder, baking soda and salt in a large bowl. Cut in the shortening with a pastry blender or fork until crumbly. Add the buttermilk mixture and stir with a fork just until moistened. Turn out onto a floured work surface and knead lightly 3 or 4 times. Roll the dough 1/2-inch thick and cut with a 2-inch biscuit cutter. Place the biscuits on a lightly greased baking sheet. Bake at 400 degrees for 10 to 12 minutes. Remove to a wire rack.

Serves 20

Interludes

Soups & Salads

Greensboro Symphony Youth Orchestra

Established in 1970 as a collaborative effort of the Greensboro Symphony Orchestra and the Guild, the Greensboro Symphony Youth Orchestra continues to thrive and grow in excellence. The Greensboro Symphony Guild currently provides both financial and volunteer assistance for the Symphony Orchestra's Youth Orchestra program. Through fund-raising initiatives the Guild offers scholarships to talented young musicians, enabling students to further their music education through both private instruction and prestigious music camps, where they study with nationally acclaimed instructors and performing artists. The Youth Orchestra has in the past been invited to perform at the Lincoln Center and at the Kennedy Center.

This program has been expanded in recent years to include beginning strings training of elementary school students in the Lillian Rauch Instrument and Loan Scholarship program at the Hampton Leadership Academy. The orchestra's beginning performers are given the opportunity to study and perform in the newly formed Allegro program designed for young musicians and the youth strings program before advancing to the Youth Orchestra.

White Spanish Gazpacho

3 cucumbers, peeled and cubed
1 small garlic clove
3 (14-ounce) cans chicken broth
3 cups sour cream
3 tablespoons white vinegar
2 teaspoons salt, or to taste
4 tomatoes, chopped
1/2 cup chopped fresh parsley
1/2 cup sliced green onions
3/4 cup sliced almonds, toasted and salted
Croutons

Purée the cucumbers and garlic in a blender. Pour into a bowl. Whisk in a small amount of chicken broth until smooth. Whisk in the remaining chicken broth gradually. Whisk the cucumber mixture gradually into the sour cream in a bowl. Stir in the vinegar and salt. Chill, covered, until cold. Ladle into 6 chilled soup bowls. Top each with equal portions of the tomatoes, parsley, green onions, almonds and croutons.

Serves 6

 For a special presentation, nestle the soup bowls in larger bowls of crushed ice.

Cincinnati Chili

4 cups water
2 pounds lean ground beef
2 large onions, chopped
1 (6-ounce) can tomato paste
2 teaspoons minced garlic
3 tablespoons chili powder
1 teaspoon black pepper
1 teaspoon cayenne pepper
1 teaspoon cumin
1 teaspoon ground cinnamon
1 teaspoon ground allspice
1 tablespoon baking cocoa
3 bay leaves
2 teaspoons Worcestershire sauce
Hot cooked spaghetti

Combine the water, ground beef, onions, tomato paste, garlic, chili powder, black pepper, cayenne pepper, cumin, cinnamon, allspice, baking cocoa, bay leaves and Worcestershire sauce in a large saucepan and mix well. Bring to a boil and cook until the ground beef is cooked through, stirring occasionally. Reduce the heat and simmer, covered, for 3 to 4 hours, stirring occasionally. Remove and discard the bay leaves. Serve over cooked spaghetti. Garnish with chopped onions and shredded Cheddar cheese.

Serves 6

Pork and Chipotle Chili

2 pounds pork tenderloin, trimmed and
    cut into 1/2-inch cubes
Salt and pepper to taste
2 tablespoons chili powder
4 slices bacon
2 cups chopped sweet onions, cut into 1/4-inch pieces
11/2 teaspoons minced garlic
1/4 cup chili powder
21/2 teaspoons oregano
5 teaspoons cumin
2 canned chipotle chiles, finely chopped
1 (14-ounce) can beef broth
11/4 cups water
11/4 cups brewed coffee
1 (14-ounce) can crushed tomatoes in tomato purée
11/2 (14-ounce) cans diced tomatoes, drained
11/2 teaspoons salt
1/4 teaspoon coarsely ground pepper
2 (15-ounce) cans black beans, drained

Season the pork with salt, pepper and 2 tablespoons chili powder. Rub the seasonings into the meat. Cook the bacon in a large heavy saucepan until crisp; drain on paper towels. Drain the bacon drippings from the saucepan. Add the pork and sauté until brown. Add the onions and garlic and sauté for 4 to 5 minutes or until tender. Add 1/4 cup chili powder, oregano, cumin and chipotle chiles and sauté for 1 minute longer. Stir in the broth, water, coffee, crushed tomatoes, diced tomatoes, salt and pepper. Simmer for 30 minutes, stirring occasionally. Adjust the seasonings to taste. Stir in crumbled bacon and black beans. Simmer for 15 to 20 minutes longer.

Serves 8

White Bean Chili

1 pound Great Northern beans
1 tablespoon olive oil
1 large onion, chopped
2 teaspoons cumin
1$^{1}/_{2}$ teaspoons oregano
Chili powder to taste
Dash of cayenne pepper
2 (4-ounce) cans chopped green chiles, undrained
4 garlic cloves, minced
6 cups chicken broth
5 cups chopped cooked chicken (about 4 breasts)
1 cup (4 ounces) shredded Monterey Jack cheese
$^{1}/_{2}$ teaspoon salt
$^{1}/_{2}$ teaspoon pepper
2 cups (8 ounces) shredded Monterey Jack cheese
$^{3}/_{4}$ cup sour cream
$^{3}/_{4}$ cup salsa
Tortilla chips
Chopped fresh parsley

Soak the beans in a saucepan of water overnight; drain and rinse. Heat the olive
oil in a large saucepan. Add the onion and sauté until tender. Add the cumin, oregano,
chili powder, cayenne pepper, green chiles and garlic and sauté for 2 minutes longer.
Stir in the beans and broth. Bring to a boil and reduce the heat. Simmer, covered, for
2 hours or until the beans are tender. Stir in the chicken, 1 cup cheese, the salt and
pepper. Bring to a boil and reduce the heat. Simmer, uncovered, for 10 minutes, stirring
frequently. Ladle into 8 soup bowls. Divide the 2 cups cheese, the sour cream and salsa
evenly among the bowls. Top with tortilla chips and chopped fresh parsley.

Serves 8

Tuscan-Style White Bean and Sausage Soup

8 ounces to 1 pound bulk Italian sausage
1/2 cup chopped onion
2 garlic cloves, minced
1/4 cup all-purpose flour
1 1/2 cups half-and-half or evaporated milk
1 (14-ounce) can chicken broth
2 (15-ounce) cans cannellini beans
Salt and pepper to taste

Brown the sausage with the onion and garlic in a saucepan, stirring until the sausage is crumbly; drain. Stir in the flour. Stir in the half-and-half and broth gradually. Bring to a boil, stirring constantly. Add the undrained beans and cook until heated through. Season with salt and pepper.

Serves 6

Pot Liquor Ham Soup

2 pounds fresh collard greens or turnip greens, trimmed and torn into 1-inch pieces
2 pounds ham steak or country ham, chopped
2 tablespoons hot red pepper sauce
3 tablespoons olive oil
3 onions, chopped
1 garlic clove, minced
6 red potatoes, chopped
3 (14-ounce) cans chicken broth
2 (16-ounce) cans field peas, drained
2 (16-ounce) cans crowder peas, drained
2 cups water
1/2 cup vermouth
1 tablespoon white vinegar
1 teaspoon salt

Cook the greens in a small amount of boiling water in a saucepan until tender; drain. Combine the ham and hot sauce in a bowl and toss well. Heat the olive oil in a large saucepan over medium-high heat. Add the ham mixture and sauté for 8 to 10 minutes or until brown. Add the onion and garlic and sauté until the onions are tender. Stir in the cooked greens, potatoes, broth, field peas, crowder peas, water, vermouth, vinegar and salt. Bring to a boil and reduce the heat. Simmer for 45 minutes, stirring occasionally.

Serves 12 to 16

Chicken Mulligatawny Soup

2/3 cup all-purpose flour
2 cups chicken broth
1/2 cup (1 stick) butter
2 onions, thinly sliced
2 cups chicken broth
2 cups canned stewed tomatoes
2 carrots, diced
2 ribs celery, diced
1 green bell pepper, diced
2 apples, cored and sliced
2 cups diced cooked chicken
1 teaspoon curry powder
Chopped fresh parsley to taste

Whisk the flour into 2 cups chicken broth in a bowl until smooth. Melt the butter in a large saucepan. Add the onions and sauté until tender. Stir in the flour mixture. Stir in 2 cups chicken broth. Stir in the tomatoes, carrots, celery, bell pepper, apples, chicken, curry powder and parsley. Simmer for 30 to 40 minutes. You may make this one day ahead. Chill, covered, overnight. This soup also freezes well.

Serves 8

Moroccan Chicken Soup

2 tablespoons butter
6 carrots, peeled and diced
5 ribs celery, diced
1 onion, diced
2 garlic cloves, crushed
8 cups chicken broth
4 cups tomato sauce
2 tablespoons grated fresh ginger
3 cinnamon sticks
Salt and pepper to taste
3 large chicken breasts, cooked, skinned, boned and diced
Cornstarch
1/2 to 3/4 cup cream or heavy cream (optional)

Melt the butter in a large saucepan. Add the carrots, celery, onion and garlic and sauté until the vegetables are tender-crisp. Stir in the broth, tomato sauce, ginger, cinnamon sticks, salt and pepper. Simmer for 30 minutes or until the vegetables are tender, stirring occasionally. Stir in the chicken. Cook for 10 minutes. Mix cornstarch and a small amount of cold water in a bowl. Stir in enough of the cornstarch mixture to thicken the soup. Cook until the soup is thickened, stirring constantly. Stir in the cream. Cook until heated through. Remove and discard the cinnamon sticks before serving.

Serves 12

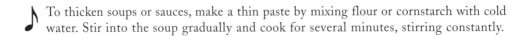 To thicken soups or sauces, make a thin paste by mixing flour or cornstarch with cold water. Stir into the soup gradually and cook for several minutes, stirring constantly.

Yucatan-Style Chicken, Lime and Orzo Soup

3/4 cup orzo
Salt to taste
4 1/2 teaspoons olive oil
1 white onion, thinly sliced
3 garlic cloves, thinly sliced
2 jalapeño chiles or roasted poblano chiles, thinly sliced
12 ounces boneless skinless chicken breasts,
    cut into thin strips
5 cups low-sodium chicken broth
1/4 cup fresh lime juice
1 large tomato, seeded and chopped
1/4 cup chopped fresh cilantro
Salt and pepper to taste

Cook the orzo in a saucepan of boiling salted water just until tender; drain. Heat the olive oil in a large saucepan over medium heat. Add the onion, garlic and chiles and sauté for 4 minutes or until the onion begins to brown. Add the chicken and sauté for 1 minute longer. Stir in the broth, lime juice and tomato. Simmer for 3 minutes or until the chicken is cooked through. Stir in the orzo, cilantro, salt and pepper and cook until heated through. Ladle into soup bowls and garnish with fresh cilantro sprigs and chopped avocado.

Serves 4

Turkey Tortilla Soup

1 tablespoon olive oil
1 large onion, chopped
1 (4-ounce) can green chiles, drained and chopped
1 large garlic clove, minced
1 teaspoon chili powder
1 teaspoon cumin
1/2 teaspoon oregano
1/4 teaspoon cayenne pepper
6 cups chicken stock
1 (16-ounce) can tomatoes, chopped
12 ounces boneless turkey breast, cut into 1/2-inch strips
Kernels from 1 ear of fresh corn, or 1 cup frozen corn kernels
1/3 cup chopped fresh cilantro (optional)
Salt and pepper to taste
1 1/3 cups shredded Monterey Jack cheese
Tortilla chips

Heat the olive oil in a large saucepan. Add the onion and sauté for 4 minutes. Add the green chiles, garlic, chili powder, cumin, oregano and cayenne pepper and sauté for 1 minute longer. Stir in the broth and tomatoes. Bring to a boil and stir in the turkey. Simmer for 15 minutes. Stir in the corn. Cook for 1 minute. Stir in the cilantro, salt and pepper. Ladle into 8 soup bowls. Divide cheese evenly among the bowls and top with tortilla chips.

You may use cooked turkey or rotisserie chicken instead of uncooked turkey and reduce the cooking time.

Serves 8

Salmon Chowder

8 ounces potatoes, peeled and cut into $1/4$-inch cubes
$2^{1}/2$ cups milk
$1/4$ teaspoon salt
2 tablespoons butter
$3/4$ cup finely chopped onion
8 ounces salmon fillets
1 tablespoon all-purpose flour
2 tablespoons chopped fresh dill weed, or
   1 teaspoon dried dill weed
1 tablespoon fresh lemon juice
$1/4$ teaspoon salt
White pepper to taste

Combine the potatoes, milk and $1/4$ teaspoon salt in a saucepan. Cook for 10 minutes or until tender. Remove from the heat. Melt the butter in a saucepan. Add the onion and sauté until tender. Lay the salmon over the onion and lay a buttered round of waxed paper over the salmon. Cook, covered, for 8 to 10 minutes, turning the salmon once during cooking. Remove the salmon with a slotted spoon to a plate and remove and discard the skin. Sprinkle the flour over the onions and cook for 3 minutes, stirring frequently. Stir in the potato mixture. Purée with an immersion blender, if desired. Cook for 5 minutes, stirring occasionally. Break the salmon into chunks and add to the soup. Stir in the dill weed, lemon juice, $1/4$ teaspoon salt and pepper. Cook over medium heat until heated through.

Serves 4

Black Bean and Bell Pepper Soup

4 cups dried black beans, rinsed
6 cups chicken stock
2 bay leaves
1 onion, finely chopped
2 large bell peppers, seeded and chopped
4 garlic cloves, minced
4 slices bacon
2 tablespoons olive oil
5 ounces smoked ham, chopped
Salt and pepper to taste

Soak the beans in a large saucepan of water overnight. Drain and return to the saucepan.
Stir in the stock and bay leaves. Simmer for 1 hour. Stir in the onion, bell peppers
and garlic. Simmer for 1 hour and 15 minutes or until the beans are tender. Cook the
bacon in the olive oil in a skillet until crisp. Remove with a slotted spoon to paper towels
to drain; crumble. Add the ham to the bacon drippings and cook over low heat for
3 minutes; drain. Add the ham and bacon to the soup and season with salt and pepper.
Cook until heated through, stirring occasionally. Remove and discard the bay leaves
before serving.

Serves 12

Asian Black Bean Soup

1 tablespoon olive oil
1 small onion, chopped
3 garlic cloves, chopped
4 (15-ounce) cans black beans
1 (14-ounce) can chicken broth
3 tablespoons soy sauce
1 teaspoon grated fresh ginger
1/2 teaspoon crushed red pepper
1/4 teaspoon coriander
1 1/2 teaspoons grated orange zest
2 tablespoons fresh orange juice
1 cup sour cream
2 tablespoons fresh orange juice
1/4 cup chopped fresh cilantro
Shredded Cheddar cheese

Heat the olive oil in a large heavy saucepan over medium heat. Add the onion and garlic and sauté for 5 minutes or until tender. Stir in the black beans, chicken broth, soy sauce, ginger, red pepper and coriander. Cook over medium heat for 20 minutes, stirring occasionally. Stir in the orange zest and 2 tablespoons orange juice. Purée half the mixture in a blender and return to the saucepan. Cook until heated through. Combine the sour cream, 2 tablespoons orange juice and cilantro in a small bowl and mix well. Ladle the soup into 8 soup bowls. Add a dollop of the sour cream mixture to each bowl and top with cheese.

Serves 8

Asparagus Soup

1 pound asparagus
1 tablespoon butter
1 (4-ounce) potato, peeled and chopped
1/4 cup chopped onion
1/2 cup chopped celery
1 garlic clove, crushed
1 sprig fresh thyme, or 1/4 teaspoon dried thyme
1 bay leaf
2 tablespoons all-purpose flour
2 tablespoons sherry
3 3/4 cups chicken broth
1/2 cup cream or heavy cream
1/4 cup chicken broth

Trim the asparagus, reserving the asparagus tips. Chop the remaining asparagus. Melt the butter in a saucepan. Add the chopped asparagus, potato, onion, celery, garlic, thyme and bay leaf and cook for 15 minutes, stirring frequently. Stir in the flour. Stir in the sherry. Stir in 3 3/4 cups chicken broth. Simmer for 45 minutes. Remove and discard the bay leaf. Purée the soup in a blender and return to the saucepan. Stir in the cream and adjust the seasonings to taste. Cook the asparagus tips in 1/4 cup chicken broth in a small saucepan until tender-crisp. Stir into the soup.

Serves 4

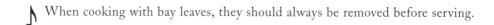 When cooking with bay leaves, they should always be removed before serving.

Broccoli Soup with Leek and Potato

3 large leeks
10 to 12 scallions
1/2 cup (1 stick) butter, cut into pieces
4 cups chicken broth
2 cups vegetable broth
Salt and pepper to taste
3 large potatoes, peeled and diced
2 bunches broccoli crowns, chopped
1 cup cream or heavy cream
1 cup half-and-half

Remove and discard the green tops of the leeks. Wash the leeks and cut in half lengthwise. Cut into 1/2-inch pieces. Remove and discard the green tops of the scallions. Wash and chop into 1/4-inch pieces. Melt the butter in an 8-quart saucepan. Add the leeks and scallions and sauté for 15 minutes or until the leeks are tender. Stir in the chicken broth, vegetable broth, salt and pepper. Simmer for 7 to 8 minutes. Stir in the potatoes and simmer for 15 minutes. Stir in the broccoli and cook over medium heat for 10 minutes. Reduce the heat and simmer for 2 minutes. Remove from the heat. Purée in batches in a blender. Return the mixture to the saucepan. Whisk in the cream and half-and-half over low heat. Cook until heated through or serve chilled as a summer soup.

Serves 10 to 12

Fresh Mushroom and Onion Soup

1 tablespoon butter
3 onions, coarsely chopped
1 tablespoon butter
1 pound mushrooms, sliced
2 tablespoons chicken bouillon granules
3 cups water
1/3 cup finely chopped fresh parsley
3 tablespoons tomato paste
1 garlic clove, crushed
1/4 teaspoon freshly ground pepper
1 cup dry white wine
Shredded Swiss cheese
Small cubes of rye bread

Melt 1 tablespoon butter in a saucepan. Add the onions and sauté until tender; do not let brown. Melt 1 tablespoon butter in a skillet. Add the mushrooms and sauté until tender; do not overcook. Add the mushrooms to the onions. Dissolve the bouillon in the water in a bowl or measuring cup. Add to the mushroom mixture. Stir in the parsley, tomato paste, garlic, pepper and wine. Cook until heated through, stirring occasionally. Place cheese in the bottom of soup bowls and ladle the soup over the cheese. Top with bread cubes.

Serves 4 to 6

Mushroom and Barley Soup with Pancetta

4 ounces pancetta or bacon, cut into 1/2-inch strips
2/3 cup chopped onion
1/2 cup chopped carrots
2 garlic cloves, minced
1 pound button mushrooms, sliced
6 shiitake mushrooms, sliced
3 cups beef broth
1/2 cup vermouth
1 1/2 cups chicken broth
1/2 cup barley, rinsed
2 cups Swiss chard or spinach (optional)
Romano cheese

Cook the pancetta in a large saucepan over medium-high heat for 6 minutes or until crisp; drain on paper towels. Remove the excess drippings from the saucepan. Add the onion, carrots and garlic and sauté for 5 minutes or until the vegetables are tender, adding olive oil if needed. Add the button mushrooms and shiitake mushrooms and sauté for 5 minutes longer. Stir in the beef broth and vermouth and let simmer. Combine the chicken broth and barley in a saucepan. Bring to a boil over medium-high heat and reduce the heat to low. Cook, covered, for 30 minutes or until the barley is tender. Add the cooked barley to the soup. Stir in the Swiss chard and cook until wilted. Garnish each serving with shavings of Romano cheese.

Serves 4 to 6

Cream of Roasted Sweet Red Pepper Soup

1 tablespoon butter
6 garlic cloves
1 small onion, chopped
2 (14-ounce) cans chicken broth
1 bay leaf
1/2 teaspoon salt
1/4 teaspoon pepper
11/2 to 2 cups chopped roasted red bell peppers
2 tablespoons butter
2 tablespoons all-purposes flour
11/2 cups cream or heavy cream
Julienned fresh basil

Melt 1 tablespoon butter in a heavy saucepan. Add the garlic and onion and sauté until tender-crisp. Stir in the broth, bay leaf, salt and pepper. Bring to a boil and reduce the heat. Simmer for 30 minutes. Remove and discard the bay leaf. Strain the soup through a wire mesh strainer into a bowl. Remove the solids to a food processor. Add the roasted bell peppers. Process for 30 seconds or until smooth, stopping once to scrape down the side. Melt 2 tablespoons butter in a large heavy saucepan over low heat. Stir in the flour. Cook for 1 minute, stirring constantly. Stir in the strained broth mixture gradually. Cook over low heat for 3 minutes or until thick and bubbly, stirring frequently. Stir in the pepper mixture. Stir in the cream gradually. Cook over low heat until heated through. Garnish with julienned fresh basil.

Serves 8

♪ To roast the bell peppers, place them on a foil-lined baking sheet. Broil 5 inches from the heat source until charred, turning to char evenly. Remove to a bowl and cover with plastic wrap. Let stand for 10 minutes. Peel and chop the peppers, removing the stems and seeds. Chill, covered, for up to 1 week, if desired. The peppers may be charred over a gas flame instead of under the broiler. You may use three 8-ounce jars of roasted red bell peppers instead.

Tomato and Smoked Gouda Soup

1 (42-ounce) can tomatoes
12 ounces smoked Gouda cheese, cut into 1-inch cubes
1/2 cup fresh basil leaves
1 (14-ounce) can chicken broth
Salt and pepper to taste

Process the tomatoes, cheese, basil and broth in a food processor or blender until the cheese is finely chopped. Pour into a saucepan. Bring to a light boil and reduce the heat to low. Simmer for 30 minutes; some of the cheese will remain unmelted. Season with salt and pepper. Serve garnished with fresh chopped parsley.

You may use one 28-ounce can diced tomatoes and one 14-ounce can tomatoes with basil, garlic and oregano instead of one 42-ounce can tomatoes.

Serves 4

Cream of Carrot Soup

1/4 cup (1/2 stick) unsalted butter
1 cup chopped onion
1 tablespoon dark brown sugar
1 tablespoon curry powder
2 teaspoons minced fresh ginger
1/2 teaspoon coriander
1/4 teaspoon cardamom
1/8 teaspoon nutmeg
1 pound carrots, peeled and chopped
2 potatoes, peeled and chopped
7 cups chicken stock
1 cup cream or heavy cream

Melt the butter over low heat in a large saucepan. Add the onion and cook for 7 minutes or until light brown, stirring occasionally. Stir in the brown sugar, curry powder, ginger, coriander, cardamom and nutmeg and cook for 1 minute. Stir in the carrots, potatoes and stock. Bring to a boil and reduce the heat. Simmer, covered, for 30 minutes or until the vegetables are tender. Purée in batches in a blender. Return the mixture to the saucepan. Stir in the cream. Cook over very low heat for 10 minutes. Adjust the seasonings to taste. Ladle into soup bowls and garnish with mint or cilantro leaves or serve chilled as a summer soup.

Serves 8

Pumpkin Soup

1/4 cup (1/2 stick) butter
1 large yellow onion, finely chopped
1 (16-ounce) can tomatoes, chopped
8 ounces carrots, peeled and cut into large chunks
2 1/2 cups chicken broth
1 (16-ounce) can pumpkin
1 1/4 cups chicken broth
Pinch of sugar
Salt and pepper to taste
2 tablespoons finely chopped fresh basil, or
   2 teaspoons dried basil
3 tablespoons cream or heavy cream (optional)

Melt the butter in a large saucepan. Add the onion and sauté for 4 to 5 minutes or until tender. Stir in the tomatoes and simmer for 5 to 6 minutes or until the tomatoes are slightly mushy.

Simmer the carrots in 2 1/2 cups broth in a saucepan until tender. Pour the carrots, broth and pumpkin into a food processor or blender. Process until smooth, adding 1 1/4 cups broth gradually to make a thin, creamy consistency. Add to the onion mixture. Stir in the sugar, salt, pepper, basil and cream. Cook until heated through; do not let boil. Ladle into soup bowls and garnish with shredded Swiss cheese and toasted pumpkin seeds or sunflower seeds.

Serves 6

Italian Chicken Salad

3 cups cubed cooked chicken breasts
1 cup chopped red bell pepper
2 tablespoons chopped fresh parsley
1 tablespoon chopped fresh oregano
1 tablespoon chopped fresh basil
12 kalamata olives, pitted and halved
1 (14-ounce) can artichoke hearts, drained and chopped
2 tablespoons olive oil
1 tablespoon red wine vinegar
4 1/2 teaspoons fresh lemon juice
1/2 teaspoon minced garlic
1/2 teaspoon sugar
1/4 teaspoon pepper
1/8 teaspoon salt

Combine the chicken, bell pepper, parsley, oregano, basil, olives and artichokes in a
large bowl. Whisk the olive oil, vinegar, lemon juice, garlic, sugar, pepper and salt in
a bowl. Add to the chicken mixture and toss gently.

Serves 4

Lemony Chicken Salad with Wild Rice and Grapes

DRESSING
1/3 cup fresh lemon juice (about 2 lemons)
2 teaspoons olive oil
1 teaspoon Dijon mustard
1/2 teaspoon salt
1/2 teaspoon freshly ground pepper

SALAD
1 (6-ounce) package wild rice (1 cup)
3 to 4 cups chicken broth
1 teaspoon herbes de Provence, or 1/8 teaspoon thyme
1/2 teaspoon salt
3/4 teaspoon freshly ground pepper
3 cups cooked chicken, cut into 1/2-inch pieces
    (11/4 pounds uncooked boneless chicken)
1 rib celery, finely chopped
8 ounces seedless red grapes, halved lengthwise
8 ounces seedless green grapes, halved lengthwise
Red leaf lettuce

For the dressing, whisk the lemon juice, olive oil, Dijon mustard, salt and pepper in a bowl.

For the salad, combine the rice, broth, herbes de Provence, salt and pepper in a saucepan. Cook according to the rice package directions. Remove the rice to a large bowl and let cool slightly. Add the chicken, celery, red grapes, green grapes and dressing and toss well. Line salad plates with lettuce. Mound the chicken salad on the lettuce. Serve warm or at room temperature.

The rice, chicken and dressing can be prepared one day ahead. Chill, covered, until ready to serve. Bring to room temperature, combine and toss when ready to serve.

Serves 6 to 8

Curried Cranberry Chicken Salad

3/4 cup light mayonnaise
1/4 cup fat-free plain yogurt
1 tablespoon lime juice
3/4 teaspoon curry powder
1/4 teaspoon salt, or to taste
White pepper to taste
3 cups cubed cooked chicken
   (1 1/4 pounds uncooked boneless
   chicken)

2/3 cup chopped celery
3 tablespoons sliced green onions or
   sweet onion
1 medium-large apple, cored and cut
   into 1/2-inch cubes
2/3 cup sweetened dried cranberries
1/2 cup toasted pecans, chopped

Combine the mayonnaise, yogurt, lime juice, curry powder, salt and pepper in a bowl and mix well. Add the chicken, celery and green onions and toss well. Chill, covered, for up to 24 hours. Add the apple, dried cranberries and pecans within 4 hours of serving and toss well. Chill until ready to serve.

Serves 6

Beach Vacation Pasta Salad

1 (16-ounce) package rotini pasta,
   cooked al dente and drained
1 (10-ounce) package frozen baby green
   peas, thawed

2 cups grape tomatoes, cut into halves
1 small red onion, coarsely chopped
3 garlic cloves, minced
4 to 5 tablespoons prepared pesto

Combine the pasta, peas, tomatoes, onion, garlic and pesto in a bowl and toss well. Chill, covered, for 1 hour. Add cooked shrimp or cooked chicken to make this salad a main dish.

Serves 12

Tuna Niçoise Pasta Salad

SALAD
8 ounces green beans, trimmed and cut into 1-inch pieces
12 ounces rotini or other corkscrew pasta
2 (6-ounce) cans white tuna, drained
5 green onions, sliced
1 large tomato, seeded and chopped
1/2 cup pitted kalamata olives, chopped

DRESSING
3/4 cup light mayonnaise
2 tablespoons balsamic vinegar
1 tablespoon lemon juice
1/2 teaspoon Dijon mustard
1/2 teaspoon celery salt (optional)
1 to 2 tablespoons drained capers
Salt and pepper to taste

For the salad, cook the green beans in a large saucepan of boiling salted water for 4 minutes or until tender-crisp. Remove the green beans with a slotted spoon to a colander to drain. Add the pasta to the boiling water in the saucepan and cook until al dente. Pour into the colander with the green beans and drain well. Place the tuna in a large bowl and break into small pieces. Add the green onions, tomato, olives, pasta and green beans.

For the dressing, whisk the mayonnaise, vinegar, lemon juice, Dijon mustard and celery salt in a small bowl. Stir in the capers, salt and pepper.

To assemble, add the dressing to the tuna mixture and toss well. Serve immediately or chill, covered, until ready to serve. Let warm slightly before serving.

Serves 8

Orzo Salad

SALAD
12 ounces orzo (about 2 cups)
1 tablespoon olive oil
1 1/2 pounds tomatoes, seeded and chopped
   (about 3 tomatoes)
1 large cucumber, peeled, seeded and chopped
6 scallions, chopped
1 cup chopped fresh parsley
6 tablespoons chopped fresh mint or basil
1/2 cup kalamata olives, pitted and sliced (optional)
1/4 cup crumbled feta cheese (optional)

DRESSING
5 tablespoons fresh lemon juice (about 2 lemons)
1 teaspoon salt
1/2 teaspoon freshly ground pepper
1/2 cup olive oil

For the salad, cook the orzo in a saucepan of boiling water until al dente. Drain well and remove to a large bowl. Add the olive oil and toss to coat. Add the tomatoes, cucumber, scallions, parsley, mint, olives and cheese and toss well.

For the dressing, whisk the lemon juice, salt, pepper and olive oil in a bowl. Add to the salad and toss to coat. Serve immediately or chill, covered, for up to 1 day to allow the flavors to blend. Let warm to room temperature before serving.

Serves 6

Crunchy Broccoli Pecan Salad

SALAD
1 (3-ounce) package ramen noodles
2 tablespoons butter
1 cup chopped pecans
1 head romaine, torn into bite-size pieces
4 cups broccoli florets
4 green onions, sliced
1 (10-ounce) package frozen green peas, thawed (optional)

DRESSING
1/2 cup vegetable oil
1/2 cup sugar
1/4 cup wine vinegar
1 tablespoon soy sauce
Salt and pepper to taste

For the salad, crumble the ramen noodles slightly and discard the seasoning packet. Melt the butter in a skillet. Add the noodles and pecans and sauté until golden brown. Remove from the heat and let cool. Combine the romaine, broccoli, green onions and peas in a large bowl and toss well. Add the noodles and pecans and toss well.

For the dressing, whisk the oil, sugar, vinegar, soy sauce, salt and pepper in a bowl. Add to the salad and toss to coat. Serve immediately.

Serves 10 to 12

Asparagus Salad with Roasted Peppers and Cheese

2 pounds asparagus, tough ends trimmed
2 red bell peppers
1 tablespoon white wine vinegar
2 tablespoons drained capers
1 tablespoon Dijon mustard
1 garlic clove, minced

3 tablespoons minced shallots
1/4 cup olive oil
Salt and freshly ground pepper to taste
12 pitted kalamata olives, chopped
Shavings of Parmigiano-Reggiano
    cheese or mild goat cheese

Cook the asparagus in a large skillet of boiling water for 3 minutes or until tender-crisp; drain. Rinse in cold water and pat dry. Roast the bell peppers (see page 84) and cut into 1/4-inch strips. Arrange the asparagus on a serving platter and top with the roasted bell pepper strips. Whisk the vinegar, capers, Dijon mustard, garlic and shallots in a bowl. Whisk in the olive oil. Season with salt and pepper. Drizzle half over the asparagus and roasted bell pepper strips. Top with the olives and cheese and pass the remaining vinaigrette.

The asparagus, roasted bell peppers and vinaigrette can be prepared up to 24 hours ahead and stored separately in sealable containers and chilled. Bring to room temperature before assembling and serving.

Serves 8

Marinated Asparagus

1 pound asparagus, trimmed
1/3 cup vinegar
1/4 cup sugar
1/4 cup water
Salt to taste

1/2 teaspoon pepper
1/4 teaspoon celery seeds
3 whole cloves
1 cinnamon stick

Cook the asparagus in a skillet of boiling water or in the microwave for 3 to 4 minutes or until tender-crisp; drain. Place in a shallow baking dish. Combine the vinegar, sugar, water, salt, pepper, celery seeds, cloves and cinnamon stick in a small saucepan. Bring to a boil. Pour over the asparagus. Chill, covered, for 24 hours, turning occasionally. Drain before serving.

Serves 6 to 8

Beet Salad with Stilton and Walnuts

1/3 cup walnut halves
2 pounds red beets or yellow beets
2 tablespoons olive oil
Salt and freshly ground pepper to taste
31/2 tablespoons extra-virgin olive oil
21/2 tablespoons red wine vinegar
2 cups mixed salad greens
3 ounces Stilton cheese, crumbled

Spread the walnuts over a baking sheet. Bake at 375 degrees for 5 to 7 minutes or until light brown and fragrant. Remove to a wire rack to cool. Rinse the beets and remove all but 1/2 inch of stem. Arrange the beets in a shallow baking dish and drizzle with 2 tablespoons olive oil. Turn the beets to coat and season with salt and pepper. Bake, covered with foil, at 375 degrees for 50 to 60 minutes or until tender. Let cool until able to handle and slip off the skins.

Cut the beets into thin wedges and place in a bowl. Whisk 31/2 tablespoons olive oil and the vinegar in a small bowl. Season with salt and pepper. Drizzle three-fourths of the vinaigrette over the warm beets and toss well. Let cool completely. Place the salad greens in a serving bowl. Drizzle with the remaining vinaigrette and toss to coat. Add the beets and season with salt and pepper and toss well. Sprinkle with the cheese and toasted walnuts.

Serves 6

Marinated Gourmet Slaw

1 head cabbage, shredded
1 Bermuda onion, thinly shredded
1/4 cup sugar
6 tablespoons vegetable oil
1/4 cup sugar
1/4 cup vinegar
1/2 teaspoon dry mustard
1/2 teaspoon celery seeds
1/2 teaspoon salt

Combine the cabbage and onion in a large bowl and mix well. Sprinkle 1/4 cup sugar over the top. Combine the oil, 1/4 cup sugar, the vinegar, dry mustard, celery seeds and salt in a saucepan. Bring to a boil, stirring occasionally. Pour evenly over the cabbage mixture. Chill, covered, for 8 hours to 3 days.

Serves 6

Mixed-Up Crunchy Cabbage Salad

4 cups shredded cabbage
1 cup thinly sliced celery
1/2 cup thinly sliced radishes
1/2 cup mayonnaise
1/2 cup sour cream
1 teaspoon salt
1/2 cup diced cucumber
1/2 cup sliced green onions
1/4 cup chopped green bell pepper
1/2 cup dry-roasted peanuts
1 tablespoon butter
2 tablespoons grated Parmesan cheese

Combine the cabbage, celery and radishes in a large bowl and mix well. Chill, covered, until just before ready to serve. Combine the mayonnaise, sour cream, salt, cucumber, green onions and bell pepper in a bowl and mix well. Chill, covered, until just before ready to serve. Brown the peanuts in the butter in a skillet. Add the mayonnaise dressing to the cabbage mixture and toss to coat. Sprinkle with the peanuts and cheese.

Serves 6 to 8

Lettuce Wedges with Party Blue Cheese Dressing

PARTY BLUE CHEESE DRESSING
2 tablespoons fresh lemon juice
3/4 teaspoon garlic powder
1/2 teaspoon salt
1/4 cup finely chopped fresh chives or green onions
1 cup sour cream
1 cup mayonnaise
1/4 cup (or more) milk
5 ounces Stilton cheese or Roquefort cheese,
    broken into small chunks

SALAD
1 head iceberg lettuce, cut into 6 wedges
6 slices bacon, crisp-cooked and crumbled
2 tomatoes or 4 plum tomatoes, seeded and diced
4 thinly sliced green onions

For the dressing, whisk the lemon juice, garlic powder, salt, chives, sour cream, mayonnaise and milk in a bowl. Fold in the cheese gently. Chill, covered, for 6 hours to 3 days.

For the salad, place one lettuce wedge on each of 6 chilled salad plates. Spoon equal amounts of dressing over each lettuce wedge. Sprinkle each serving with the bacon, tomatoes and green onions. Store any remaining dressing in the refrigerator in a container with a tight-fitting lid and use as a dip.

Serves 6

Spanish Salad de Oro

1 (16-ounce) can garbanzo beans, drained and rinsed
1 (16-ounce) can black beans, drained and rinsed
1 (16-ounce) can kidney beans, drained and rinsed
1 (16-ounce) can yellow whole kernel corn
1 (2-ounce) can sliced black olives, drained
1 (4-ounce) jar diced pimentos, drained
1 (6-ounce) jar marinated artichoke hearts,
   coarsely chopped
1 yellow bell pepper, coarsely chopped
1 green bell pepper, coarsely chopped
1 onion, coarsely chopped
1 teaspoon minced garlic, or to taste
1/2 cup lemon juice
1/4 cup olive oil

Combine the garbanzo beans, black beans, kidney beans, corn, olives, pimentos, artichoke hearts with marinade, yellow bell pepper, green bell pepper, onion and garlic in a large bowl and toss well. Whisk the lemon juice and olive oil in a small bowl. Add to the bean mixture and toss well. Chill, covered, for 4 hours before serving.

Serves 15 to 20

Green Bean Feta Salad

1$1/2$ pounds green beans, cut into 2-inch pieces
3 tablespoons fresh lemon juice
3 tablespoons white wine vinegar
1 tablespoon Dijon mustard
1 teaspoon basil
$1/2$ teaspoon sugar
$1/4$ teaspoon salt
$1/4$ teaspoon pepper
1 garlic clove, minced
$1/2$ cup olive oil
$1/2$ cup chopped red onion
4 ounces feta cheese, crumbled
$1/2$ cup toasted walnuts, chopped

Cook the green beans in a saucepan of boiling water until tender-crisp. Drain and plunge into ice water until cold. Drain and pat dry. Whisk the lemon juice, vinegar, Dijon mustard, basil, sugar, salt, pepper and garlic in a large bowl. Whisk in the olive oil. Add the green beans and toss well. Spread over a serving platter. Sprinkle with the onion, cheese and walnuts.

Serves 8

Cucumber and Feta Cheese Salad

DRESSING
1/4 cup fresh lemon juice
1/4 cup olive oil
Salt and freshly ground pepper to taste

SALAD
1 large cucumber
1 cup (4 ounces) crumbled feta cheese
2 green onions, sliced
1/3 cup chopped fresh flat-leaf parsley
1 tablespoon chopped fresh dill weed, or 1 teaspoon dried dill weed
1 tablespoon chopped fresh mint (optional)
Leaf lettuce
Cherry tomatoes

For the dressing, whisk the lemon juice, olive oil, salt and pepper in a bowl.

For the salad, peel the cucumber, if desired. Halve lengthwise, remove the seeds and slice the cucumber. Place the cucumber slices in a bowl. Add the cheese, green onions, parsley, dill weed, mint and dressing and toss well. Chill, covered, until ready to serve. Line salad plates with lettuce. Spoon the salad on the lettuce and top with cherry tomatoes.

Serves 4

Hot Potato Greens

3 pounds new potatoes, quartered
2 tablespoons olive oil
1 teaspoon fines herbes
2 tablespoons chopped fresh rosemary
1/2 teaspoon garlic salt
1/2 teaspoon freshly ground pepper
1 pound bacon, cut into 1-inch pieces
1/4 cup vegetable oil
1/4 cup red wine vinegar
2 tablespoons sugar
1/2 teaspoon salt
1/2 teaspoon freshly ground pepper
2 garlic cloves, pressed
1 (10-ounce) package fresh spinach
1 (10-ounce) package mixed salad greens
6 ounces grated Parmesan cheese

Combine the potatoes, olive oil, fines herbes, rosemary, garlic salt and pepper in a bowl and toss gently. Spread over the bottom of a lightly greased 10×15-inch baking pan. Bake at 400 degrees for 30 to 40 minutes or until the potatoes are tender and light brown. Remove from the oven and keep warm.

Cook the bacon in batches in a skillet until crisp; drain on paper towels. Remove all but 1/4 cup of the bacon drippings from the skillet. Whisk the vegetable oil, vinegar, sugar, salt, pepper and garlic into the skillet. Cook over medium heat for 3 to 4 minutes, whisking occasionally. Combine the spinach, salad greens, cheese and hot dressing in a large serving bowl and toss well. Top with the potatoes and bacon and serve immediately.

Serves 6 to 8

Layered Potato Salad

6 large Idaho potatoes, peeled and cut into small pieces
1¹/2 cups mayonnaise
1 cup sour cream
1¹/2 teaspoons horseradish
¹/2 teaspoon salt
1 large sweet onion, finely chopped
1 cup chopped fresh parsley
4 large ribs celery, finely chopped

Cook the potatoes in a large saucepan of boiling water until tender; drain well. Spread half the potatoes over the bottom of a large serving dish or 9×12-inch baking dish. Combine the mayonnaise, sour cream, horseradish and salt in a bowl and mix well. Spread half the mayonnaise mixture over the potatoes in the serving dish. Sprinkle with the onion and half the parsley. Top with the remaining potatoes and the remaining mayonnaise mixture. Sprinkle with the celery and the remaining parsley. Chill, covered, overnight. Do not stir before serving.

Serves 12

Tarragon Spinach Salad

DRESSING
1/2 cup olive oil
1/4 cup sugar
3 tablespoons ketchup
2 tablespoons tarragon vinegar
1 teaspoon Worcestershire sauce
1/2 teaspoon salt
1 teaspoon finely chopped onion

SALAD
1 (9-ounce) package fresh baby spinach
1 cup fresh bean sprouts
2 hard-cooked eggs, chopped
6 slices bacon, crisp-cooked and crumbled
1/2 cup chopped green onions (optional)
1 can water chestnuts, drained, rinsed and
    diced (optional)

For the dressing, combine the olive oil, sugar, ketchup, vinegar, Worcestershire sauce, salt and onion in a jar with a tight-fitting lid and shake well.

For the salad, combine the spinach, bean sprouts, eggs, bacon, green onions and water chestnuts in a large bowl and toss well. Add the dressing and toss to coat.

Serves 6

Spinach Bacon Salad with Maple Mustard Dressing

MAPLE MUSTARD DRESSING
1/4 cup maple syrup
3 tablespoons white wine vinegar
1 tablespoon extra-virgin olive oil
1 tablespoon Dijon mustard
1/4 teaspoon salt
1/4 teaspoon freshly ground pepper

SALAD
4 slices bacon
1 large shallot, chopped
1/2 cup thinly sliced green onions
1/2 cup finely chopped red bell pepper
2 (7-ounce) packages fresh baby spinach
1 (15-ounce) can Great Northern beans, drained,
    rinsed and heated (optional)

For the dressing, whisk the maple syrup, vinegar, olive oil, Dijon mustard, salt and pepper in a microwave-safe bowl. Microwave on High for 1 minute or until hot. Keep warm.

For the salad, cook the bacon in a skillet until crisp. Remove with a slotted spoon to paper towels to drain; crumble. Add the shallot and sauté until tender. Remove to paper towels to drain. Combine the bacon, shallot, green onions, bell pepper, spinach, hot beans and hot dressing in a large bowl and toss well. Serve immediately.

Serves 6

Tangy Yellow Squash Salad

DRESSING
1/2 cup cider vinegar
1/3 cup olive oil
2 teaspoons wine vinegar
1/2 cup sugar
1 garlic clove, minced
1 teaspoon pepper

SALAD
5 to 7 yellow squash, sliced
1 green bell pepper, chopped
1/2 cup sliced green onions
2 ribs celery, sliced

For the dressing, combine the cider vinegar, olive oil, wine vinegar, sugar, garlic and pepper in a jar with a tight-fitting lid and shake well.

For the salad, combine the squash, bell pepper, green onions and celery in a large bowl and toss gently. Add the dressing and toss gently to coat. Chill, covered, for at least 2 hours.

You may use zucchini instead of yellow squash, red bell pepper instead of green bell pepper or red onion instead of green onions.

Serves 10

Waldorf Sweet Potato Salad

DRESSING
3 tablespoons apple juice
2 tablespoons vegetable oil
4 teaspoons white wine vinegar
1 teaspoon sugar
1/2 teaspoon salt

SALAD
1/3 cup chopped walnuts, toasted
3 cups grated peeled sweet potatoes
1 apple, cored and coarsely chopped
1/2 cup chopped celery
1/2 cup seedless red grapes, cut into halves
1/3 cup crumbled blue cheese (optional)
Red leaf lettuce (optional)

For the dressing, whisk the apple juice, oil, vinegar, sugar and salt in a small bowl.

For the salad, combine the walnuts, sweet potatoes, apple, celery, grapes and cheese in a large bowl and toss well. Add the dressing and toss to coat. Serve over red leaf lettuce.

Serves 8

 To toast nuts, spread in a single layer over a baking sheet or in a pie plate. Bake at 350 degrees for 5 to 10 minutes or until light brown, watching carefully so that the nuts don't burn.

Stacked Tomato Salad with Tapenade and Basil

TAPENADE
2 cups pitted kalamata olives
3 garlic cloves
2 tablespoons pine nuts
1/2 teaspoon anchovy paste
1/4 cup olive oil
Salt and pepper to taste

SALAD
1/4 cup white wine vinegar
1 tablespoon fresh lemon juice
2 tablespoons honey
1 tablespoon Dijon mustard
3/4 cup olive oil
12 large fresh basil leaves, thinly sliced
8 to 10 large tomatoes, cored and
   cut into 1/2-inch slices
2 (8-ounce) balls mozzarella cheese,
   cut into 1/4-inch slices

For the tapenade, process the olives, garlic, pine nuts and anchovy paste in a food processor until finely chopped. Add the olive oil gradually, pulsing to a thick paste. Remove to a bowl and season with salt and pepper. Chill, covered, for up to 2 days, if desired.

For the salad, whisk the vinegar, lemon juice, honey and Dijon mustard in a bowl. Whisk in the olive oil gradually. Stir in the basil. Lay 1 tomato slice on each of 8 salad plates. Spread each slice with 1 tablespoon of the tapenade. Top with a cheese slice. Repeat the layers and top with a tomato slice. Drizzle the basil dressing equally over the tomato stacks.

Alternating red and yellow tomato slices makes for an attractive presentation.

Serves 8

Tuscan Bread and Tomato Salad

1 loaf unsliced very firm white bread
4 cups grape tomatoes, cut into halves
3 tablespoons high-quality
   balsamic vinegar

3 tablespoons olive oil
3 tablespoons chopped fresh basil
1/2 teaspoon salt
1/2 teaspoon freshly ground pepper

Cut the bread into 1/2- to 3/4-inch cubes to make 4 to 6 cups of bread cubes. Spread over a large platter and let dry for several hours. Combine the bread cubes and tomatoes in a large bowl. Whisk the vinegar, olive oil, basil, salt and pepper in a small bowl. Add to the bread mixture and toss well. Serve immediately.

Serves 6 to 8

Apple Celery Salad

DRESSING
2 tablespoons cider vinegar
2 teaspoons Dijon mustard
1 teaspoon caraway seeds
1/4 cup vegetable oil
2 tablespoons finely chopped
   fresh parsley
Salt and pepper to taste

SALAD
4 ribs celery, cut into thin sticks
4 ounces smoked Swiss cheese,
   Gouda cheese or provolone cheese,
   cut into thin sticks
2 Granny Smith apples, cored and
   thinly sliced
Leaf lettuce

For the dressing, process the vinegar, Dijon mustard and caraway seeds in a blender until well mixed. Add the oil gradually, processing until well mixed. Remove to a bowl and stir in the parsley, salt and pepper.

For the salad, combine the celery, cheese and two-thirds of the dressing in a bowl and mix well. Chill, covered, for a few hours. Combine the apples and remaining dressing in a bowl and mix well. Chill, covered, for a few hours. Arrange lettuce on four chilled salad plates. Divide the apple slices evenly among the plates and fan the slices. Top evenly with the celery and cheese. Drizzle the dressing remaining in the bowls over the salad.

Serves 4

 Wrapping unused celery ribs in foil before refrigerating extends the shelf life of the celery.

Blue Cheese and Apple Vinaigrette Salad

VINAIGRETTE
1/2 cup vegetable oil
1/4 cup sugar
1/4 cup cider vinegar
1/2 teaspoon paprika
1/4 teaspoon dry mustard
1/4 teaspoon salt

SALAD
6 to 8 cups mixed salad greens
1 red onion, cut into rings
2 large Granny Smith apples, cored and chopped
4 ounces blue cheese, crumbled
1/2 cup toasted pecans, chopped (optional)

For the vinaigrette, combine the oil, sugar, vinegar, paprika, dry mustard and salt in a jar with a tight-fitting lid and shake well.

For the salad, combine the salad greens, onion, apples, blue cheese and pecans in a large bowl and toss well. Pour the dressing evenly over the salad and serve immediately.

You may use chopped pears or sliced strawberries instead of chopped apples.

Serves 6 to 8

Grape Cherry Nut Salad

DRESSING

1/3 cup frozen limeade concentrate or lemonade
  concentrate, thawed
1/3 cup honey
1/3 cup vegetable oil
1 teaspoon celery seeds or poppy seeds

SALAD

2 cups seedless green grapes
4 ribs celery, chopped (about 2 cups)
1 cup pitted dark sweet cherries, cut into halves
1/2 cup coarsely chopped nuts, toasted
Leaf lettuce

For the dressing, combine the limeade concentrate, honey, oil and celery seeds in a bowl.
Beat with a rotary beater until well mixed.

For the salad, combine the grapes, celery, cherries and nuts in a bowl. Add 1/4 cup
dressing, or to taste, and toss well. Serve the salad in lettuce-lined salad bowls. Store
any remaining dressing in the refrigerator in a container with a tight-fitting lid and
save for another use.

Serves 6

Orange and Grapefruit Salad

DRESSING
2 tablespoons sugar
1/4 teaspoon salt
2 tablespoons malt vinegar
2 tablespoons vegetable oil
1/8 teaspoon almond extract

SALAD
3 oranges, peeled, seeded and sectioned
1 grapefruit, peeled, seeded and sectioned
1/2 cup chopped celery
2 tablespoons sliced green onions
Mixed salad greens

For the dressing, whisk the sugar, salt, vinegar, oil and almond extract in a small bowl.

For the salad, combine the oranges, grapefruit, celery and green onions in a bowl. Add the dressing and toss well. Serve over mixed greens.

Serves 4

Strawberry and Romaine Salad

SALAD
Butter
1/4 cup sliced almonds
Salt to taste
1 head romaine, torn into bite-size pieces
2 cups fresh strawberries, sliced
1 red onion, thinly sliced

DRESSING
2 cups mayonnaise
2/3 cup sugar
1/3 cup light cream
1/3 cup raspberry vinegar
2 tablespoons poppy seeds
2 to 3 tablespoons raspberry jam

For the salad, melt a small amount of butter in a skillet. Add the almonds and sauté until lightly toasted. Remove to paper towels to drain. Sprinkle with salt and let cool. Combine the almonds, romaine, strawberries and onion in a large bowl.

For the dressing, whisk the mayonnaise, sugar, cream, vinegar, poppy seeds and jam in a bowl. Add enough dressing to the salad to coat and toss well. Serve immediately. Store the remaining dressing in the refrigerator in a container with a tight-fitting lid and use with other fruit salads.

Serves 6

Wheat Berry Waldorf Salad

2 cups soft wheat berries
7 cups water
1 cup chopped walnuts, toasted
2 Granny Smith apples or Gala apples, cored and chopped
1 cup raisins
3/4 cup sweetened dried cranberries
3/4 cup chopped dried apricots
1 cup finely chopped fresh parsley
1/2 cup extra-virgin olive oil
1/4 cup cider vinegar
1/4 cup apple juice
2 tablespoons lemon juice
1 tablespoon salt
1 teaspoon sugar
1/2 teaspoon freshly ground pepper
1/2 teaspoon nutmeg
1/2 teaspoon ground cinnamon

Add enough water to cover the wheat berries by a few inches in a bowl. Let soak for 6 to 8 hours or overnight; drain. Bring 7 cups water to a boil in a saucepan. Add the wheat berries. Simmer for 50 minutes or until tender but still chewy. Drain and let cool. Combine the cooled wheat berries, walnuts, apples, raisins, dried cranberries, apricots and parsley in a large bowl. Whisk the olive oil, vinegar, apple juice, lemon juice, salt, sugar, pepper, nutmeg and cinnamon in a bowl. Add to the salad and toss well. Adjust the seasonings to taste. Chill, covered, for up to 3 days.

Serves 10 to 12

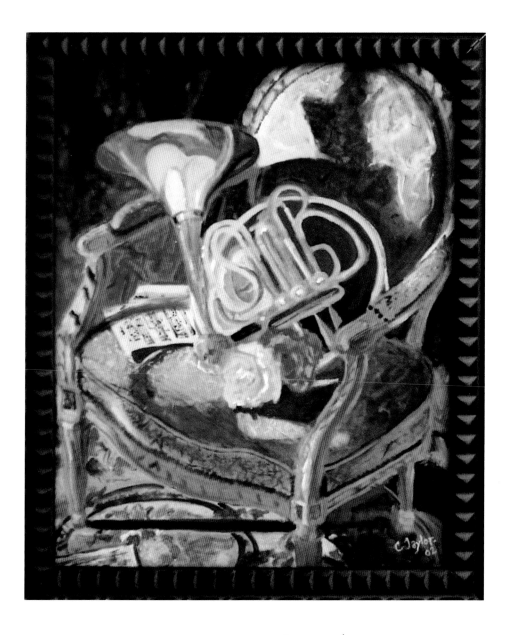

Accompaniments
Vegetables & Sides

Community Outreach

The Guild's service to the orchestra and community can be illustrated by its involvement in the orchestra's outreach programs. The Guild provides financial and volunteer backing for Preludes, educational programs offered by local musical educators preceding classical concerts and featuring a discussion of masterworks included in the evening's program. In addition, the Guild provides funding for Music at Midday programs presented by Greensboro Symphony Orchestra ensembles at area retirement homes. The Guild's Women's Chorus, which performs for many local organizations throughout the year, is perhaps the organization's most visible goodwill ambassador for the musical arts. Recent marketing efforts have resulted in the newly formed Speakers Bureau, a Web site (www.gsoguild.org), and the Advocacy Committee. These new initiatives have provided avenues for increasing community awareness of Guild activities and support of music education on the local, state, and federal levels.

Guild member and artist Christine Taylor generously provided this oil painting titled Parlor Music *for a recent Homes Tour raffle. Born in Scotland, she enjoys painting musical instruments in a variety of settings; one of her works, painted when she was just seven years old, hangs in the Paisley Museum of Art in her native country.*

Baked Artichokes

2 (14-ounce) cans quartered artichokes,
    drained and patted dry
1 tablespoon fresh lemon juice
2 tablespoons freshly grated Parmesan cheese
1 teaspoon Italian seasoning, or $3/4$ teaspoon oregano
3 tablespoons finely chopped pecans (optional)
1 garlic clove, minced
2 teaspoons olive oil

Spread the artichokes over the bottom of a 9-inch pie plate coated with nonstick cooking spray. Sprinkle evenly with the lemon juice. Combine the cheese, Italian seasoning, pecans, garlic and olive oil in a small bowl and mix well. Sprinkle evenly over the artichokes. Bake at 375 degrees for 15 minutes or until the topping is golden brown.

Serves 6

Roasted Asparagus with Balsamic Butter

2 tablespoons butter
2 teaspoons soy sauce
1 teaspoon balsamic vinegar
Olive oil
40 asparagus spears, trimmed (about 2 pounds)
$1/4$ teaspoon kosher salt or sea salt
$1/8$ teaspoon coarsely ground pepper

Melt the butter in a small skillet over medium heat. Cook for 3 minutes or until light brown, shaking the skillet occasionally. Remove from the heat and stir in the soy sauce and vinegar. Keep warm. Coat a foil-lined 10×15-inch baking pan with olive oil or nonstick cooking spray. Arrange the asparagus in a single layer over the baking pan. Sprinkle with the salt and pepper. Bake at 400 degrees for 12 minutes or until tender. Drizzle the butter mixture over the asparagus and toss well to coat. Serve immediately.

Serves 8

Asparagus Casserole

12 to 16 thick slices dry dense white bread
2 1/2 to 3 cups milk
1 to 1 1/2 pounds asparagus, trimmed and
    cut into 2-inch pieces
5 eggs
1 teaspoon salt
1 teaspoon pepper
1/2 cup chopped fresh chives, parsley, tarragon and/or
    a mixture of the herbs
4 ounces shredded Swiss cheese
4 ounces shredded fontina cheese
1/4 cup (1 ounce) grated Romano cheese
1 tablespoon butter, cut into small pieces

Arrange the bread in a single layer in a shallow dish. Pour the milk evenly over the bread. Soak for 30 minutes or until the milk is absorbed. Press on the bread and remove the excess milk to a measuring cup. Add additional milk if needed to make 1/2 cup. Set the milk and soaked bread aside. Place the asparagus in a steamer rack over boiling water in a saucepan. Steam for 2 to 3 minutes or until tender-crisp. Remove to a colander and rinse under cold water; drain. Remove and reserve 6 to 8 asparagus tips. Combine the eggs, salt, pepper and 1/2 cup reserved milk in a bowl and beat well.

Place one-third of the soaked bread in a buttered 3-quart soufflé dish. Top with half of the asparagus, half the herbs, one-third of the Swiss cheese, one-third of the fontina cheese and one-third of the Romano cheese. Repeat the layers, using one-third of the bread, the remaining asparagus, remaining herbs, one-third of the Swiss cheese, one-third of the fontina cheese and one-third of the Romano cheese. Top with the remaining bread and sprinkle with the remaining Swiss cheese, fontina cheese and Romano cheese. Arrange the reserved asparagus tips on the top. Pour the egg mixture evenly over the layers and dot with the butter. Bake at 350 degrees for 45 minutes or until the top is golden brown and a knife inserted near the center comes out clean.

Serves 8 to 10

Creamy Orzo with Asparagus and Prosciutto

2 tablespoons butter
2 ounces thinly sliced prosciutto, cut into thin strips
2 tablespoons butter
1¼ cups (8 ounces) orzo
3 cups chicken broth
1 pound thin asparagus, cut into 1-inch pieces
⅓ cup freshly grated Parmesan cheese
Salt and pepper to taste

Melt 2 tablespoons butter in a large nonstick saucepan or skillet over medium-high heat. Add the prosciutto and sauté for 3 minutes or until almost crisp. Remove with a slotted spoon to paper towels to drain. Add 2 tablespoons butter to the saucepan and melt over high heat. Add the orzo and sauté for 1 minute. Stir in the broth. Bring to a boil and reduce the heat to medium-low. Simmer, covered, for 8 minutes or until the orzo begins to soften, stirring occasionally. Stir in the asparagus. Simmer, covered, for 3 minutes or until the asparagus is tender-crisp. Simmer, uncovered, for 1 minute or until almost all the liquid is absorbed. Remove from the heat and stir in the prosciutto, cheese, salt and pepper. Garnish with shavings of Parmesan cheese.

Serves 6

♪ To make shavings of Parmesan cheese or chocolate, use a vegetable peeler.

Eggplant Parmigiana

3/4 cup all-purpose flour
2 teaspoons salt
1/3 cup milk
1 large eggplant, cut into 1/4-inch slices
2 to 3 tablespoons vegetable oil (or more)
1 (16-ounce) jar spaghetti sauce
Sautéed bell peppers, onion, garlic and mushrooms (optional)
1 cup ricotta cheese
1/2 cup (2 ounces) grated Parmesan cheese
8 ounces shredded mozzarella cheese

Mix the flour and salt together on a sheet of waxed paper. Pour the milk into a shallow
dish. Dip the eggplant slices into the milk and coat in the flour mixture. Heat the oil in
a skillet over medium heat. Sauté the eggplant a few slices at a time until golden brown,
adding more oil, if needed. Remove the eggplant to paper towels to drain. Combine the
spaghetti sauce and bell peppers, onion, garlic and mushrooms in a bowl and mix well.
Spread a layer of the sauce over the bottom of a greased 12×12-inch baking dish. Top
with some of the eggplant, some of the ricotta cheese, some of the Parmesan cheese
and some of the mozzarella cheese. Continue layering to use all of the sauce, eggplant,
ricotta cheese, Parmesan cheese and mozzarella cheese, ending with the mozzarella
cheese. Bake at 350 degrees for 25 minutes or until heated through. This may be frozen
before baking. Thaw and bring to room temperature before baking.

Serves 6

Green Beans Provençal

2 slices bacon
1/2 cup chopped onion
1/2 cup chopped celery (optional)
1 pound green beans, sliced
1 teaspoon salt
1/8 teaspoon pepper
1/2 teaspoon oregano
2 to 3 Roma tomatoes, coarsely chopped

Cook the bacon in a large skillet until crisp; drain on paper towels and crumble. Remove all but 2 tablespoons of the bacon drippings from the skillet. Add the onion and celery and sauté until the vegetables are tender. Stir in the green beans, salt, pepper and oregano. Cook, covered, for 5 minutes, stirring occasionally. Stir in the tomatoes. Cook for 5 minutes or until the green beans are tender. Sprinkle with the bacon.

Serves 4

Steamed Chinese Green Beans

1 tablespoon peanut oil
2 drops of sesame oil
1 tablespoon tamari or soy sauce
1 teaspoon rice vinegar or cider vinegar
1/2 garlic clove, crushed
Pinch of sugar
8 ounces green beans, cut into 6-inch pieces

Whisk the peanut oil, sesame oil, tamari, vinegar, garlic and sugar in a small bowl. Place the green beans in a steamer rack over boiling water in a saucepan. Steam for 3 to 5 minutes or until tender-crisp. Remove the green beans to a bowl. Add the oil mixture to the hot green beans and toss well to coat. Let cool to room temperature.

Serves 4

Green Beans with Shiitake Mushrooms

2 pounds French green beans or thin green beans, trimmed
3 tablespoons butter
8 ounces shiitake mushrooms, stemmed and sliced
2 tablespoons butter
2 shallots, minced
2 garlic cloves, minced
Salt and pepper to taste

Cook the green beans in a saucepan of boiling water for 3 to 5 minutes or until tender-crisp. Remove to a colander and rinse under cold water; drain. Melt 3 tablespoons butter in a large skillet over medium-high heat. Add the mushrooms and sauté for 5 minutes. Remove to a bowl. This may all be prepared 1 to 2 hours in advance.

Add 2 tablespoons butter to the skillet. Add the shallots and garlic and sauté for 2 minutes. Add the green beans and mushrooms. Cook until heated through, tossing frequently. Season with salt and pepper.

Serves 8

Green Beans with Warm Mustard Vinaigrette

2 shallots, minced
2 tablespoons Dijon mustard
2 tablespoons balsamic vinegar
1/2 cup extra-virgin olive oil
Salt and freshly ground pepper to taste
2 pounds green beans, trimmed
1/4 cup chopped fresh dill weed

Combine the shallots, Dijon mustard, vinegar, olive oil, salt and pepper in a small saucepan. Cook just until hot, whisking constantly. Keep warm. Cook the green beans in a large saucepan of boiling water for 2 to 3 minutes or until tender-crisp; drain well. Add the warm vinaigrette to the hot green beans and toss well to coat. Add the dill weed and toss well. Serve immediately.

Serves 8

Broccoli with Balsamic Butter

2 tablespoons balsamic vinegar
2 tablespoons dry red wine
6 tablespoons chilled unsalted butter, cut into small pieces
Salt and freshly ground pepper to taste
1 large bunch broccoli, trimmed and separated into florets

Mix the vinegar and wine in a small saucepan. Cook over medium-high heat until reduced by half. Remove from the heat and whisk in the butter gradually. Whisk until the mixture is creamy. Season with salt and pepper. Cover to keep warm. Place the broccoli in a steamer rack over boiling water in a saucepan. Steam just until tender-crisp. Remove the broccoli to a bowl. Add the butter mixture and toss well to coat. Serve immediately.

Serves 4 to 6

Broccoli à la Orange

2 tablespoons butter
2 tablespoons all-purpose flour
1/2 teaspoon grated orange zest
1/2 cup orange juice
1/2 cup orange sections
1/4 teaspoon salt
1/4 teaspoon tarragon (optional)
1/2 cup plain yogurt
1 1/2 pounds broccoli crowns, separated into florets

Melt the butter in a saucepan. Stir in the flour. Cook for 1 minute, stirring constantly. Stir in the orange zest, orange juice, orange sections, salt and tarragon. Cook until bubbly and thickened, stirring often. Stir in the yogurt. Keep warm. Place the broccoli in a steamer rack over boiling water in a saucepan. Steam just until tender-crisp. Remove the broccoli to a serving platter. Spoon the warm orange sauce over the broccoli.

Serves 6

Shredded Brussels Sprouts with Caraway Seeds

2 cups brussels sprouts, trimmed
3 tablespoons vegetable oil
1 teaspoon caraway seeds
2 tablespoons red wine vinegar
Pinch of sugar
1 slice bacon, crisp-cooked and crumbled

Cut the brussels sprouts in half lengthwise and thinly slice. Heat the oil in a skillet. Add the brussels sprouts and caraway seeds and sauté until tender-crisp and light brown. Remove from the heat and stir in the vinegar and sugar. Remove to a serving dish and sprinkle with the bacon. Serve immediately.

Serves 2

Baby Carrots with Dill and Capers

1 pound baby carrots, trimmed and lightly peeled
Salt to taste
1/4 cup (1/2 stick) unsalted butter, melted
1/4 cup chopped fresh dill weed
1 1/2 tablespoons finely chopped capers

Cook the carrots in a saucepan of boiling salted water just until tender; drain well. Add the melted butter, dill weed and capers to the hot carrots and toss well to coat.

Serves 6

Mustard-Glazed Carrots

6 cups sliced carrots
1/4 cup (1/2 stick) butter
1/2 cup packed brown sugar
1/4 cup yellow mustard
1/2 teaspoon salt
2 tablespoons chopped fresh parsley

Cook the carrots in a saucepan of boiling water for 10 to 15 minutes or until tender; drain well. Melt the butter in a large saucepan. Stir in the brown sugar, mustard and salt. Cook until the sugar is dissolved, stirring constantly. Add the carrots and cook until the carrots are glazed, stirring constantly. Remove to a serving dish and sprinkle with the parsley.

Serves 8 to 10

Southwestern Corn Pudding

1 (12-ounce) can yellow whole kernel corn, drained, or
   1 (10-ounce) package frozen corn, thawed
2 tablespoons all-purpose flour
2 tablespoons sugar
2 tablespoons butter, softened
1 teaspoon salt
2 eggs, beaten
1 green bell pepper or red bell pepper, chopped
4 green onions, chopped
1 (4-ounce) can chopped green chiles (optional)
1/8 teaspoon ground cinnamon (optional)
1 cup (4 ounces) shredded Mexican-style cheese
   (Cheddar and Monterey Jack blend)
1/2 cup half-and-half or milk

Combine the corn, flour, sugar, butter, salt, eggs, bell pepper, green onions, green chiles, cinnamon, cheese and half-and-half in a bowl and mix well. Pour into a buttered 1-quart baking dish. Bake at 350 degrees for 30 to 40 minutes or until thickened and golden brown.

Serves 6

Peas with Spinach and Shallots

1 tablespoon vegetable oil
1 tablespoon unsalted butter
2 shallots, thinly sliced
2 garlic cloves, thinly sliced
1 (10-ounce) package frozen green peas

1/4 cup water
5 ounces fresh baby spinach
3/4 teaspoon salt
1/4 teaspoon pepper

Heat the oil and butter in a nonstick 12-inch skillet over medium heat. Add the shallots and garlic and sauté for 6 minutes or until tender. Stir in the peas and water. Cook, covered, for 5 minutes or until the peas are tender, stirring occasionally. Add the spinach, salt and pepper. Cook for 1 minute or just until the spinach is wilted, tossing constantly.

Serves 4

Fancy Peas

2 tablespoons butter
1 cup sliced fresh mushrooms
1/4 cup finely chopped onion
1/4 teaspoon nutmeg
1/8 teaspoon marjoram
2 tablespoons sherry

1/4 teaspoon salt
Freshly ground pepper
1 (10-ounce) package frozen
    green peas, cooked according
    to the package directions

Melt the butter in a saucepan. Add the mushrooms and onion and sauté for 5 minutes. Stir in the nutmeg, marjoram, sherry, salt, pepper and hot peas. Adjust the seasonings to taste.

Serves 4

Saucy Mushrooms

4 slices turkey bacon, chopped
1 tablespoon olive oil
1 pound fresh white mushrooms,
    1 1/2 to 2 inches in diameter
2 tablespoons stone-ground mustard
2 tablespoons chopped fresh parsley

Cook the bacon in a large heavy skillet until crisp. Remove with a slotted spoon to
paper towels to drain. Add the olive oil to the bacon drippings and heat until hot.
Add the mushrooms and sauté for 1 to 2 minutes or just until starting to brown.
Reduce the heat. Cook, covered, for 8 minutes or until the mushrooms are tender,
stirring occasionally. Stir in the bacon and mustard. Sprinkle with the parsley
before serving.

Serves 4

Oven-Fried Seasoned Potatoes

2 pounds large Idaho potatoes or sweet potatoes,
   peeled and cut lengthwise into wedges
1 to 2 tablespoons olive oil
1/2 teaspoon salt
1/4 teaspoon thyme
1/4 teaspoon pepper
1/8 teaspoon nutmeg

Combine the potatoes, olive oil, salt, thyme, pepper and nutmeg in a bowl and toss
well to coat. Spread in a single layer over a 10×15-inch baking pan coated with nonstick
cooking spray. Bake on the bottom rack in the oven at 450 degrees for 25 minutes or
until crisp on the outside and tender on the inside, turning once.

Serves 4 to 6

Wasabi Mashed Potatoes

1 tablespoon wasabi powder
3/4 cup milk
3 pounds russet potatoes, peeled and
    cut into 2-inch pieces
Salt to taste
1/4 cup (1/2 stick) butter
Pepper to taste

Dissolve the wasabi powder in the milk in a small bowl. Cover the potatoes with cold salted water in a saucepan. Bring to a boil and cook for 20 minutes or until tender. Drain well and remove to a bowl. Add the wasabi mixture and butter. Beat with an electric mixer until smooth and fluffy. Season with salt and pepper.

These potatoes can be prepared up to 2 hours ahead. Cover and let stand at room temperature. Reheat in the microwave before serving.

Serves 6

Creamy Potato Gruyère Gratin

1 teaspoon butter
1 garlic clove, cut into halves
3 cups cream or heavy cream
1¹/₂ teaspoons kosher salt
¹/₈ teaspoon freshly grated nutmeg
¹/₈ teaspoon white pepper
¹/₈ teaspoon cayenne pepper
4 Idaho potatoes (2 pounds), peeled
2¹/₂ cups (10 ounces) grated Gruyère cheese

Grease a 10-cup gratin dish with the butter. Rub the inside of the dish with the garlic halves. Discard the garlic. Combine the cream, salt, nutmeg, white pepper and cayenne pepper in a large bowl and mix well. Slice the potatoes paper thin on a mandoline and add to the cream mixture as sliced. Add the cheese and mix well. Pour into the prepared dish, making sure the potato slices are level and flat.

Place the gratin dish in a larger baking pan. Add enough hot water to the larger pan to come three-quarters up the side of the gratin dish, creating a bain-marie. Bake on the center rack of the oven at 350 degrees for 2 hours or until set and golden brown on top.

Serves 6 to 8

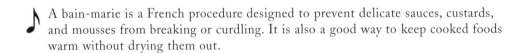 A bain-marie is a French procedure designed to prevent delicate sauces, custards, and mousses from breaking or curdling. It is also a good way to keep cooked foods warm without drying them out.

Scalloped Potatoes with Apples

3³/4 cups cream or heavy cream
2 garlic cloves, minced
1³/4 teaspoons salt
1/2 teaspoon freshly ground pepper
1/4 cup horseradish, drained
2³/4 pounds Idaho potatoes, peeled and thinly sliced
1¹/2 large Granny Smith apples, peeled, halved, cored and thinly sliced
1/4 cup (1 ounce) freshly grated Parmesan cheese

Combine the cream, garlic, salt and pepper in a bowl and mix well. Stir in the horseradish gradually, adjusting the amount to taste. Arrange three layers of potatoes in a 9×13-inch baking dish. Spread the apples over the potatoes. Top with the remaining potatoes. Pour the cream mixture evenly over the top. Bake in the upper third of the oven at 400 degrees for 30 minutes or until bubbly. Sprinkle with the cheese. Bake for 15 minutes longer or until the potatoes are tender and the top is golden brown. Remove from the oven and cover with foil. Let stand in a warm place for 10 to 30 minutes. Cut into squares and serve.

These potatoes can be prepared up to two hours ahead. Let stand at room temperature before baking.

Serves 12

Layered Sweet Potato Casserole

5 large sweet potatoes
2 seedless oranges, thinly sliced
3/4 cup orange juice
1/4 cup (1/2 stick) butter
1/2 cup packed brown sugar
1/2 teaspoon ground cinnamon

Cook the potatoes in a saucepan of boiling water until almost tender; drain. Peel the potatoes when cool enough to handle and cut into 1/2-inch slices. Arrange the potatoes in an overlapping layer in a baking dish. Insert an orange slice between every 3 or 4 potato slices. Mix the orange juice, butter, brown sugar and cinnamon in a saucepan. Bring to a boil and reduce the heat. Simmer for 5 to 10 minutes, stirring occasionally. Pour the hot syrup evenly over the potatoes and oranges. Bake at 350 degrees for 30 to 45 minutes. This can be made ahead. Chill, covered, until ready to bake. Bring to room temperature before baking.

Serves 6 to 8

Roasted Sweet Potatoes with Rosemary Honey Vinaigrette

5 cups cubed peeled sweet potatoes
1 tablespoon extra-virgin olive oil
1/4 cup honey
3 tablespoons white wine vinegar
1 tablespoon extra-virgin olive oil
3 tablespoons chopped fresh rosemary (do not use dried)
2 garlic cloves, minced
1/2 teaspoon salt
1/2 teaspoon freshly ground pepper

Combine the potatoes and 1 tablespoon olive oil in a bowl and toss well to coat. Spread in a single layer over a foil-lined 10×15-inch baking pan coated with nonstick cooking spray. Bake at 450 degrees for 35 minutes or until light brown; do not stir. Whisk the honey, vinegar, 1 tablespoon olive oil, the rosemary, garlic, salt and pepper in a bowl. Add the potatoes and toss well to coat. Serve hot or at room temperature.

Serves 6

Super Onions

4 ounces shredded mozzarella cheese
4 ounces shredded Colby cheese
1 cup (or more) herb-seasoned stuffing
1/4 cup chopped chives
2 sweet onions, very thinly sliced
1 bunch green onions, sliced
1/2 teaspoon salt
Freshly ground pepper to taste
1/4 cup dry sherry

Combine the mozzarella cheese, Colby cheese and 1 cup stuffing in a bowl and mix well. Combine chives, sweet onions and green onions in a bowl and mix well. Alternate layers of the cheese mixture with the onion mixture in a 2-quart baking dish. Sprinkle with the salt and pepper. Drizzle evenly with the sherry. Top with additional stuffing, if desired. Bake, covered, at 350 degrees for 45 minutes. Bake, uncovered, for 15 minutes longer.

Serves 6

Mostaccioli Spinach Bake

3 tablespoons butter
1 cup sliced onion
2 teaspoons minced garlic
1/4 cup all-purpose flour
2 1/2 cups milk
1/4 cup (1 ounce) grated Parmesan cheese
1 1/2 teaspoons Italian seasoning
1/2 teaspoon pepper
8 ounces mostaccioli pasta, cooked al dente and drained
1 cup (4 ounces) grated Parmesan cheese
1 (14-ounce) can tomatoes with garlic, basil and oregano
1 (10-ounce) package frozen chopped spinach,
   thawed and squeezed dry
1 tablespoon butter, melted
2 tablespoons freshly grated Parmesan cheese
1/4 cup dry bread crumbs

Melt 3 tablespoons butter in a saucepan. Add the onion and garlic and sauté until tender. Add the flour and cook until the flour is light brown, stirring constantly. Stir in the milk slowly. Cook until bubbly, stirring constantly. Stir in 1/4 cup cheese, the Italian seasoning and pepper. Pour into a large bowl. Add the pasta, 1 cup cheese, the tomatoes and spinach and mix well. Spread into a buttered 9×13-inch baking dish. Combine 1 tablespoon butter, 2 tablespoons cheese and bread crumbs in a small bowl and mix well. Sprinkle over the pasta mixture. Bake at 350 degrees for 30 minutes.

Serves 6

Spinach and Artichokes en Casserole

1 (9-ounce) package frozen artichoke hearts, thawed
Sliced water chestnuts (optional)
2 (10-ounce) packages frozen chopped spinach,
    cooked, drained and squeezed dry
1/2 cup (1 stick) butter, melted
8 ounces cream cheese, softened
1 teaspoon lemon juice
Cracker crumbs
Butter

Arrange the artichoke hearts in a greased casserole. Top with water chestnuts. Combine the spinach, 1/2 cup melted butter, the cream cheese and lemon juice in a bowl and mix well. Pour evenly over the artichoke hearts. Sprinkle with cracker crumbs and dot with butter. Bake at 350 degrees for 25 minutes. This can be made ahead. Chill, covered, until ready to bake. Bring to room temperature before baking.

Serves 6

Garlic-Creamed Spinach

1 tablespoon olive oil
1 tablespoon butter
1 large onion, chopped
4 garlic cloves, minced
2 tablespoons all-purpose flour
3/4 cup half-and-half or sour cream
1/4 teaspoon nutmeg (optional)
1/4 teaspoon salt
Freshly ground pepper
2 (10-ounce) packages frozen chopped spinach,
   cooked and well drained
1 cup (4 ounces) freshly grated Parmesan cheese (optional)

Heat the olive oil and butter in a saucepan. Add the onion and garlic and sauté until tender. Add the flour. Cook for several minutes, stirring constantly. Remove from the heat and stir in the half-and-half, nutmeg, salt and pepper. Stir in the spinach. Return the saucepan to the heat and cook until bubbly, stirring constantly. Remove from the heat and stir in half the cheese. Adjust the seasonings to taste. Sprinkle with the remaining cheese before serving.

Serves 6

Acorn Squash Filled with Pears

3 acorn squash
1/2 cup (1 stick) butter
2 onions, finely chopped
Salt and pepper to taste
2 large pears, peeled, cored and cut into 1/4-inch cubes
1/2 teaspoon ginger
1/2 teaspoon mace
3 tablespoons brown sugar
3 tablespoons bourbon
3 tablespoons sweetened dried cranberries (optional)

Cut the squash in half lengthwise and remove the seeds. Place the squash, cut side up, in a baking dish. Add enough hot water to come 1 inch up the sides of the baking dish. Cover with foil. Bake at 400 degrees for 25 to 30 minutes.

Melt the butter in a skillet. Add the onions and sauté until tender and golden brown. Season with salt and pepper. Stir in the pears, ginger, mace, brown sugar, bourbon and dried cranberries. Cook for 3 minutes, stirring constantly. Spoon the pear mixture into the squash cavities. Bake, covered, at 400 degrees for 10 minutes.

Serves 6

♪ Some feel that mace has a strong taste. Nutmeg may be substituted for a milder flavor.

Butternut Squash with Shallots

2 tablespoons olive oil
3 large shallots, halved and cut into
  $1/4$-inch slices (about $3/4$ cup)
1 ($13/4$-pound) butternut squash, peeled, seeded and
  cut into $1/2$-inch cubes (about 4 cups)
$1/2$ cup chicken broth or water
1 tablespoon brown sugar
$1/2$ teaspoon finely chopped fresh sage
$1/2$ teaspoon salt
1 teaspoon balsamic vinegar
$1/4$ teaspoon pepper

Heat the olive oil in a heavy 12-inch skillet over medium heat. Add the shallots and squash and sauté for 5 minutes or until the shallots are tender. Add the broth, brown sugar, sage and salt. Stir until the sugar is dissolved. Simmer, covered, for 8 to 10 minutes or until the squash is tender, stirring occasionally. Remove from the heat and stir in the vinegar and pepper. Adjust the seasonings to taste.

Serves 4

 Butternut squash is easily peeled with a vegetable peeler. Use a grapefruit spoon to remove the seeds.

Sherry Cherry Tomatoes

2 tablespoons extra-virgin olive oil
3 large garlic cloves, minced
1 small onion, finely chopped
2 cups cherry tomatoes or grape tomatoes
2 tablespoons sherry vinegar or dry sherry
1 teaspoon sugar
1/2 teaspoon crushed red pepper flakes
Salt to taste

Heat an ovenproof skillet over medium-high heat. Add the olive oil, garlic and onion and sauté for 2 to 3 minutes. Stir in the tomatoes. Add the vinegar, sugar, red pepper flakes and salt and toss well to coat. Bake at 375 degrees for 18 to 20 minutes.

Serves 4

Baked Tomato with Asparagus

24 asparagus spears, trimmed
4 large tomatoes, halved crosswise and cored
1 cup mayonnaise
2 cups (8 ounces) shredded sharp Cheddar cheese
2 dashes of hot red pepper sauce
3 tablespoons grated onion
1 tablespoon Dijon mustard

Place the asparagus spears in a steamer rack over boiling water in a saucepan. Steam until tender-crisp. Remove to a work surface. Cut the asparagus spears to fit the top of the tomatoes. Save the cut pieces of the asparagus spears for another use. Arrange the tomatoes, cut side up, in a buttered 9×13-inch baking dish. Top each tomato half with 3 asparagus spears. Combine the mayonnaise, cheese, hot sauce, onion and Dijon mustard in a bowl and mix well. Spoon evenly over the tomatoes and asparagus. Bake at 350 degrees for 10 to 15 minutes or until heated through.

This can be made ahead. Chill, covered, until ready to bake. Bring to room temperature before baking.

Serves 8

Broiled Tomatoes

6 tomatoes
1/2 cup plain or Italian-style bread crumbs
1/4 cup (1 ounce) grated Parmesan cheese
1 tablespoon finely chopped chives or green onions
1/4 cup finely chopped fresh parsley
1/2 teaspoon salt
1/2 teaspoon pepper
1/4 cup (1/2 stick) butter, melted

Cut the tomatoes in half crosswise. Hold the halves upside down over the sink and squeeze gently to remove the seeds. Place the tomato halves, cut side up, in a buttered baking dish. Combine the bread crumbs, cheese, chives, parsley, salt, pepper and melted butter in a bowl and mix well. Spoon equal amounts over the top of each tomato half. Broil for 5 to 6 minutes or until very hot and golden brown on top.

Serves 6 to 12

Scalloped Tomatoes

8 tomatoes, cored and cut into 1/2-inch-thick slices
1/4 teaspoon salt
1 tablespoon balsamic vinegar
1 cup fresh bread crumbs
1 large garlic clove, minced
1 1/2 tablespoons chopped fresh thyme
1/4 teaspoon freshly ground pepper
1/4 teaspoon salt
1 tablespoon extra-virgin olive oil

Arrange the tomato slices in a slightly overlapping layer in a lightly oiled 2-quart shallow baking dish. Sprinkle with 1/4 teaspoon salt and drizzle evenly with the vinegar. Combine the bread crumbs, garlic, thyme, pepper and 1/4 teaspoon salt in a bowl and mix well. Sprinkle over the tomatoes. Drizzle the olive oil evenly over the bread crumb mixture. Bake at 425 degrees for 20 to 30 minutes or until the tomatoes are tender and the topping is crisp and golden brown. Serve hot.

This recipe tastes best with garden fresh tomatoes.

Serves 8

Tomato Grits

2 cups water
1¼ cups milk
1 teaspoon salt
1 cup quick-cooking grits
½ cup (1 stick) butter, cut into pieces
1 tablespoon butter
⅓ cup chopped green onions
4 ounces Velveeta cheese, cubed
¼ teaspoon garlic powder
1½ cups (6 ounces) shredded Cheddar cheese
1 (10-ounce) can tomatoes with green chiles
1 cup (4 ounces) shredded Cheddar cheese

Bring the water and milk to a boil in a large saucepan. Add the salt and gradually add
the grits, stirring constantly. Bring to a boil and cook for 1 minute, stirring constantly.
Stir in ½ cup butter and cook until the butter is melted. Reduce the heat. Cook, covered,
for 3 to 5 minutes or until the grits are thick and creamy. Remove from the heat.

Melt 1 tablespoon butter in a skillet. Add the green onions and sauté for 1 minute. Add
the green onions, Velveeta cheese, garlic powder and 1½ cups Cheddar cheese to the
hot grits. Stir until the cheese is melted. Add the tomatoes with green chiles and mix
well. Pour into a greased 8×11-inch baking dish. Bake at 350 degrees for 35 minutes.
Sprinkle with 1 cup Cheddar cheese and bake 5 minutes longer.

Serves 8

Roasted Winter Vegetables

Salt to taste
8 ounces rutabaga, peeled and cut into pieces
8 ounces carrots, peeled and cut into pieces
8 ounces parsnips, peeled and cut into pieces
8 ounces brussels sprouts, trimmed
8 ounces sweet potatoes, peeled and cut into pieces
1 tablespoon unsalted butter
1 tablespoon extra-virgin olive oil
2 teaspoons chopped fresh thyme
2 teaspoons chopped fresh sage
1/8 teaspoon freshly grated nutmeg
Pepper to taste
1/2 cup marsala or chicken broth

Fill a large saucepan three-quarters full with salted water. Bring to a boil and add the rutabaga, carrots and parsnips. Simmer for 4 minutes or until the vegetables give slightly when pierced with a fork. Drain well and remove to a large roasting pan. Add the brussels sprouts and sweet potatoes.

Melt the butter in a small saucepan over low heat. Add the olive oil, thyme, sage and nutmeg and mix well. Pour over the vegetables in the roasting pan and toss well to coat. Spread the vegetables evenly in the pan and season with salt and pepper. Add the marsala along the edges of the pan. Cover the pan tightly with foil. Bake at 450 degrees for 40 minutes. Toss the vegetables to mix. Bake, uncovered, for 20 to 30 minutes longer or until the marsala has evaporated and the vegetables are tender. Remove the vegetables to a warm platter and serve immediately.

Serves 6

Summer Vegetable Gratin

1 zucchini, cut into 1/4-inch-thick slices (1 1/4 cups)
1 to 2 yellow squash, cut into 1/4-inch-thick slices (1 1/4 cups)
1 large leek or onion, cut into 1/4-inch-thick slices (1 cup)
1 tablespoon olive oil
Salt and pepper to taste
1 tablespoon olive oil
2 tablespoons Italian-style bread crumbs
1/4 cup (1 ounce) freshly grated Parmesan cheese
2 teaspoons chopped fresh thyme
1 garlic clove, minced

Combine the zucchini, yellow squash, leek, 1 tablespoon olive oil, salt and pepper in a bowl and toss well to coat. Spoon into a 2-quart baking dish lightly coated with nonstick cooking spray. Combine 1 tablespoon olive oil, the bread crumbs, cheese, thyme and garlic in a bowl and mix well. Sprinkle evenly over the vegetables. Bake, covered, at 425 degrees for 10 minutes. Bake, uncovered, for 10 minutes longer or until the vegetables are tender.

Serves 4

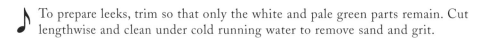 To prepare leeks, trim so that only the white and pale green parts remain. Cut lengthwise and clean under cold running water to remove sand and grit.

Barley Pilaf

1/2 cup (1 stick) butter
2 onions, chopped
12 ounces mushrooms, trimmed and sliced
1 1/2 cups pearl barley
3 jarred pimentos, coarsely chopped
2 cups chicken broth
Salt and pepper to taste

Melt the butter in a saucepan. Add the onions and mushrooms and sauté until the mushrooms are golden brown and tender. Add the barley and sauté until the barley is light brown. Remove to a baking dish. Stir in the pimentos, broth, salt and pepper. Bake, covered, at 350 degrees for 50 to 60 minutes or until the barley is tender and the liquid is absorbed.

This can be made ahead. Chill, covered, until ready to bake. Bring to room temperature before baking. Serve with game.

Serves 8

 Pearl barley is barley that has been steamed and polished after the hulls are removed.

Wild Rice and Cranberry Pilaf

3/4 cup wild rice, rinsed and drained
3 cups chicken broth
1/2 cup pearl barley
1/4 cup chopped sweetened dried cranberries,
    dried apricots or dried tart cherries
1/4 cup dried currants
1 tablespoon butter
1/3 cup sliced almonds, toasted

Combine the wild rice and broth in a saucepan. Bring to a boil and reduce the heat. Simmer, covered, for 10 minutes. Remove from the heat and stir in the barley, dried cranberries, dried currants and butter. Pour into a 1 1/2-quart baking dish. Bake, covered, at 325 degrees for 55 to 60 minutes or until the wild rice and barley are tender and the liquid is absorbed, stirring once during baking. Fluff with a fork and stir in the almonds.

Serves 6

Brown Rice and Pine Nut Casserole

2 tablespoons butter
1/2 cup pine nuts
2 tablespoons butter
1 cup brown rice, rinsed and drained
1/2 cup bulgur (cracked wheat)
1 large onion, chopped
3/4 cup finely chopped fresh parsley
6 tablespoons finely chopped chives or scallions
1/4 teaspoon salt
1/4 teaspoon pepper
3 (14-ounce) cans beef broth or chicken broth
1/4 cup finely chopped fresh parsley

Melt 2 tablespoons butter in a skillet over medium heat. Add the pine nuts and cook for 5 minutes or until golden brown, stirring occasionally. Add 2 tablespoons butter, rice, bulgur and onion. Cook for 10 minutes, stirring frequently. Spoon into a 2-quart casserole. Stir in 3/4 cup parsley, the chives, salt and pepper. Heat the broth in a saucepan to boiling. Stir into the rice mixture. Bake, uncovered, at 375 degrees for 1 hour and 15 minutes. Sprinkle with 1/4 cup parsley and serve.

Serves 6 to 8

Baked Risotto Primavera

1 tablespoon extra-virgin olive oil
2 onions, chopped (about 1 1/2 cups)
1 cup short grain or medium grain brown rice
3 garlic cloves, minced
1/2 cup dry white wine
2 (14-ounce) cans chicken broth, or
    3 1/2 cups vegetable broth
8 ounces asparagus, trimmed and
    cut into 1-inch pieces (2 cups)
1 cup sugar snap peas or snow peas, trimmed and
    cut into 1-inch pieces
1 cup diced red bell pepper or
    jarred roasted red bell peppers
3 ounces freshly grated Parmesan cheese
1/2 cup chopped fresh parsley (optional)
1/4 cup chopped green onions
1 to 2 teaspoons grated lemon zest
Freshly ground pepper to taste

Heat the olive oil in a Dutch oven or deep ovenproof sauté pan over medium heat. Add the onions and cook for 3 to 5 minutes or until tender, stirring occasionally. Add the rice and garlic and sauté for 1 minute longer. Stir in the wine and simmer until most of the wine has evaporated. Stir in the broth and bring to a boil. Bake, covered, at 425 degrees for 45 to 60 minutes or just until the rice is tender.

Shortly before the rice is done, place the asparagus, peas and bell pepper in a steamer rack over boiling water in a saucepan. Steam for 4 minutes or until the vegetables are tender-crisp. Fold the steamed vegetables, cheese, parsley, green onions, lemon zest and pepper into the hot rice and serve immediately.

Serves 4 to 6

Lemon Basil Risotto with Tomato Topping

TOPPING
1¹/2 cups chopped seeded tomatoes
2 tablespoons chopped green onions
1¹/2 teaspoons extra-virgin olive oil
1 teaspoon balsamic vinegar
¹/4 teaspoon crushed red pepper
Dash of sugar
Dash of salt
Dash of freshly ground black pepper

RISOTTO
¹/2 teaspoon salt
¹/4 teaspoon freshly ground pepper
¹/8 teaspoon nutmeg

3 cups fat-free reduced-sodium
   chicken broth
2 tablespoons butter
1 cup chopped onion
1¹/2 cups arborio rice
2 garlic cloves, minced
¹/2 cup dry white wine
1 cup fat-free reduced-sodium
   chicken broth
1 cup (4 ounces) grated
   Parmesan cheese
1 teaspoon grated lemon zest
3 tablespoons fresh lemon juice
¹/3 cup finely chopped fresh basil

For the topping, combine the tomatoes, green onions, olive oil, vinegar, red pepper, sugar, salt and black pepper in a bowl and mix well. Let stand, covered, at room temperature.

For the risotto, add the salt, pepper and nutmeg to 3 cups broth and heat to boiling. Melt the butter in a 6-quart saucepan over medium heat. Add the onion and sauté for 2 minutes. Add the rice and garlic and sauté for 2 minutes. Add the wine and cook for 1 minute or until the wine has evaporated, stirring frequently. Add ¹/2 cup seasoned broth and cook until the broth is absorbed, stirring constantly. Continue adding the seasoned broth, ¹/2 cup at a time. Cook until the broth is absorbed before adding more, stirring constantly. Heat 1 cup broth to boiling. Add ¹/2 cup of the hot broth to the risotto and cook until the broth is absorbed, stirring constantly. Stir in the remaining ¹/2 cup hot broth if necessary for a creamy consistency and tender but firm rice. Fold in the cheese, lemon zest, lemon juice and basil. Serve with the tomato topping. The risotto is also delicious on its own.

Serves 6

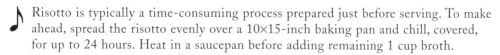 Risotto is typically a time-consuming process prepared just before serving. To make ahead, spread the risotto evenly over a 10×15-inch baking pan and chill, covered, for up to 24 hours. Heat in a saucepan before adding remaining 1 cup broth.

Lemon Rice

5 1/3 tablespoons butter
1 cup thinly sliced celery
1 small onion, finely chopped
2 cups trimmed and sliced mushrooms (optional)
1/4 teaspoon thyme
1 1/2 teaspoons salt
1/8 teaspoon white pepper
1 1/2 cups water
Grated zest of 1 lemon (about 2 teaspoons)
1/2 cup fresh lemon juice
1 cup long grain white rice

Melt the butter in a heavy 12- to 14-inch skillet over low heat. Add the celery, onion and mushrooms and sauté for 5 minutes. Stir in the thyme, salt and pepper. Remove from the heat. Combine the water, lemon zest and lemon juice in a 2-quart saucepan and bring to a boil. Add the rice and vegetable mixture. Bring to a boil and stir. Reduce the heat to low. Simmer, covered, for 20 minutes.

For a stronger lemon flavor, increase the lemon juice and reduce the water, keeping the total amount of liquid to 2 cups.

Serves 6 to 8

♪ This rice is a delicious stuffing for trout or salmon or as an accompaniment for fish and poultry.

Lemon Orzo with Peas

3 cups water
1¹/₂ cups orzo
¹/₂ teaspoon salt
1 cup frozen tiny green peas, thawed
2 tablespoons butter
2 teaspoons grated lemon zest
2 tablespoons fresh lemon juice
1 tablespoon finely chopped fresh mint or basil

Bring the water to a boil in a saucepan. Stir in the orzo and salt and reduce the heat to medium. Cook, covered, for 8 to 10 minutes or until the orzo is al dente. Add the peas and cook for 2 minutes longer. Drain any excess water. Add the butter, lemon zest and lemon juice and mix well. Sprinkle with the mint and serve immediately.

Serves 6

Slow-Cooker Macaroni and Cheese

8 ounces macaroni
1 1/3 cups milk
1 (5-ounce) can evaporated milk
1/4 cup (1/2 stick) butter
1 cup (4 ounces) shredded mozzarella cheese
1 cup (4 ounces) shredded Cheddar cheese
1 cup sour cream
1 teaspoon salt
1/4 teaspoon pepper
1/2 teaspoon dry mustard (optional)
1 cup (4 ounces) shredded mozzarella cheese
1 cup (4 ounces) shredded Cheddar cheese

Cook the macaroni in a saucepan of boiling water for 5 to 7 minutes. Drain, rinse
and drain well. Remove to a large bowl. Add the milk, evaporated milk, butter, 1 cup
mozzarella cheese, 1 cup Cheddar cheese, the sour cream, salt, pepper and dry mustard
and mix well. Pour into a slow cooker coated with nonstick cooking spray. Top with
1 cup mozzarella cheese and 1 cup Cheddar cheese. Cook on High for 2 hours or Low
for 4 to 5 hours. This recipe may be doubled.

Serves 6

Fettuccini with Shiitake Mushrooms and Basil

2 tablespoons extra-virgin olive oil or chicken broth
3 garlic cloves, minced
2 ounces shiitake mushrooms, stemmed and
   sliced (about 1 1/2 cups)
2 teaspoons grated lemon zest
2 tablespoons fresh lemon juice
1/4 teaspoon salt, or to taste
Freshly ground pepper to taste
8 ounces fettuccini or spaghetti pasta
1/4 cup chopped fresh basil
1/2 cup (2 ounces) freshly grated Parmesan cheese
1/4 cup chopped fresh basil

Heat the olive oil in a large nonstick skillet over low heat. Add the garlic and sauté for 1 minute or until fragrant but not brown. Add the mushrooms and increase the heat to medium-high. Cook for 4 to 5 minutes or until the mushrooms are tender and light brown, stirring occasionally. Stir in the lemon zest, lemon juice, salt and pepper and remove from the heat.

Add the pasta to a large saucepan of lightly salted boiling water. Cook for 9 to 11 minutes or until al dente; drain, reserving 1/2 cup of the cooking liquid. Add the pasta, reserved liquid and 1/4 cup basil to the mushroom mixture and toss well. Sprinkle with the cheese and 1/4 cup basil and serve immediately.

Serves 8 as a side dish or 4 as a main course

Almond Vegetable Topping

1/2 cup (1 stick) butter, softened
1/4 cup sliced or slivered almonds, toasted
1 tablespoon honey
1 drop of almond extract

Combine the butter, almonds, honey and almond extract in a bowl and mix well. Toss with hot cooked carrots or a hot cooked green vegetable.

Serves 12

Ranch House Potato Dressing

2 cups cottage cheese
1 cup cream or heavy cream
1 tablespoon grated onion
2 tablespoons paprika
1 teaspoon Worcestershire sauce
1/2 teaspoon salt
1/4 teaspoon garlic powder
1 teaspoon MSG (optional)

Process the cottage cheese, cream, onion, paprika, Worcestershire sauce, salt, garlic powder and MSG in a food processor until thickened and smooth. Serve over baked potatoes or as a dip with potato chips.

Serves 16

Artichoke Salsa

1 (14-ounce) can artichoke hearts, drained and chopped
3 Roma tomatoes, seeded and diced
1/3 cup diced red onion or sweet onion
8 kalamata olives, pitted and diced
1 tablespoon capers, drained and rinsed
1/2 teaspoon salt
1/2 teaspoon pepper
2 tablespoons chopped fresh basil or oregano
1/4 cup olive oil
3 tablespoons balsamic vinegar
Feta cheese

Combine the artichoke hearts, tomatoes, onion, olives, capers, salt, pepper, basil, olive oil and vinegar in a bowl and mix well. Let stand at room temperature for 2 to 4 hours. Serve with grilled fish and garnish with feta cheese.

Serves 10

Fruit Salsa

1 mango or peach, diced
1/2 red onion, diced
1 large red bell pepper, diced
Juice of 1 lime
1/2 teaspoon sugar
1/4 cup chopped fresh cilantro

Combine the mango, onion and bell pepper in a bowl. Whisk the lime juice, sugar and cilantro in a small bowl. Add to the fruit just before serving and toss well. Serve over grilled, broiled or pan-fried fish or with pork or chicken.

Serves 10

Rhubarb Currant Chutney

3/4 cup packed dark brown sugar
1/3 cup cider vinegar
2 tablespoons water
1 tablespoon minced fresh ginger
1 1/2 teaspoons grated lemon zest
1 cinnamon stick
2 cups chopped fresh rhubarb
1/2 cup currants
Salt to taste

Combine the brown sugar, vinegar, water, ginger, lemon zest and cinnamon stick in a heavy saucepan and mix well. Bring to a boil, stirring to dissolve the sugar. Stir in the rhubarb and currants and reduce the heat. Simmer for 5 minutes or until the rhubarb is tender. Season with salt. Remove and discard the cinnamon stick. Pour into a bowl. Chill, covered, for up to 1 week. Serve with roast pork, ham, turkey or chicken.

Serves 6

Blueberry Chipotle Chutney

4 cups fresh blueberries
1 cup finely chopped cored peeled Granny Smith apple
1/2 cup white wine vinegar
1/3 cup sugar
1/3 cup honey
4 1/2 teaspoons grated orange zest
4 1/2 teaspoons grated lemon zest
1 tablespoon mustard seeds
1 tablespoon chopped canned chipotle chile
   in adobo sauce (about 1 chile)
1/2 teaspoon salt
1/2 teaspoon ginger

Combine the blueberries, apple, vinegar, sugar, honey, orange zest, lemon zest, mustard seeds, chipotle chile, salt and ginger in a large saucepan and mix well. Bring to a boil and reduce the heat. Simmer for 25 minutes or until thickened, stirring frequently. It will continue to thicken as it cools. Remove from the heat. Pour into airtight containers when cool. Store in the refrigerator for up to 2 months. Serve with chicken or pork or spoon over cream cheese, goat cheese or Brie cheese as an appetizer.

Serves 32

♪ Store leftover chipotle chiles in a glass container in the refrigerator for up to 3 months. Remove the seeds from the chiles for less heat.

Brandied Cranberry Sauce

1 (12-ounce) package fresh cranberries, rinsed and drained
1¹/2 cups sugar
¹/3 to ¹/2 cup brandy
2 tablespoons finely shredded orange zest

Combine the cranberries, sugar, brandy and orange zest in an 8×8-inch or 9×9-inch baking dish and mix well. Bake at 325 degrees for 1 hour or until the cranberries are tender and most of the liquid has evaporated, stirring occasionally. Serve warm or chilled. This can be made up to one week ahead. Chill, covered, until ready to serve.

Serves 10

Cranberry Orange Sauce

1 pound (4 cups) fresh cranberries, rinsed and drained
2¹/2 cups sugar
1 cup walnuts, coarsely chopped and toasted
1 cup orange marmalade
Juice of 1 large lemon

Combine the cranberries and sugar in a shallow baking pan and toss well. Cover with foil. Bake at 350 degrees for 30 to 40 minutes or until the sugar is dissolved, stirring occasionally. Remove to a bowl. Stir in the walnuts, orange marmalade and lemon juice. Chill, covered, for up to 3 weeks.

Serves 20

Wagner — Overture to *Rienzi*
Daniel Asia — Cello Concerto
World Premiere
Mr. Brey
Intermission
Beethoven — Symphony No. 6 in F Major, Op. 68, *Pastorale*
Allegro ma non troppo
Andante molto moto
Allegro
Allegro

Season Sponsor
US Airways
Greensboro

Media Sponsors: The News & Record and WUNC
Flowers are provided by
Will & Julia Roach (Saturday) and Herbert Winfield Reich (Monday)

M. FICKETT

Masterworks

Meats, Poultry & Seafood

Support of GSO

For forty-one years the Guild has enthusiastically worked with the Symphony in developing effective ticket campaigns, securing special contributions, selling playbill ads, and working in the United Arts Council Fund Drive. Guild members have the opportunity to meet orchestra members and guest artists ten times per year by preparing and serving meals to the orchestra during rehearsals.

To ensure the continued excellence of the Symphony, in May 1986 the Guild established the Endowment Fund with a commitment to endow the $250,000 Concertmaster's Chair, payment on which was completed in May 1995. Today's Endowment Fund has a value of over $3 million and has contributed more than $1 million in earned income to support the orchestra and its education programs.

Greensboro artist and Guild member Maggie Fickett is a native of Maine and received her art training in Boston. She specializes in watercolors of private homes, landscapes, and street scenes and particularly enjoys the challenge of working on location. Pictured here is a sketch done on a playbill during a symphony performance.

Roanoke Beef Tenderloin

1 (3½-pound) beef tenderloin, trimmed
1 tablespoon thyme
1 teaspoon white pepper
1 teaspoon garlic salt
1 tablespoon seasoned salt
½ teaspoon oregano
¾ teaspoon salt (optional)
1 cup water
¼ cup Worcestershire sauce

Place the tenderloin on a large piece of heavy-duty foil. Rub the thyme evenly over the meat. Combine the pepper, garlic salt, seasoned salt, oregano and salt in a bowl and mix well. Sprinkle over all sides of the meat. Seal the foil around the meat and place in a roasting pan. Chill overnight. Let stand at room temperature for 1 hour before cooking. Open the foil and pour the water and Worcestershire sauce over the meat. Roast at 400 degrees for 35 minutes or to 125 degrees on a meat thermometer for rare to medium-rare. Let stand for 10 minutes before slicing. You may cook the tenderloin on a grill instead of in the oven.

Serves 8 to 10

 When roasting boneless cuts such as tenderloin or top loin, the roasting time is determined by the meat diameter, not the length or weight. A 3-pound tenderloin will take the same time to roast as a 5-pound tenderloin.

Sautéed Beef Fillets in Wine Sauce

6 (1½-inch-thick) beef tenderloin steaks
½ teaspoon salt
1 teaspoon freshly ground pepper
2 tablespoons olive oil
1 (10-ounce) can beef broth

1 cup dry red wine
2 garlic cloves, pressed
3 tablespoons green peppercorns
¼ cup (½ stick) unsalted butter,
   cut into pieces

Sprinkle the steaks evenly with the salt and pepper. Heat a sauté pan over high heat and add the olive oil. Add the steaks and brown on both sides. Remove the steaks to a plate. Cover with foil and keep warm. Add the broth, wine and garlic to the sauté pan. Cook over high heat for 15 minutes, scraping any brown bits from the bottom of the pan. Add the steaks and cook for 5 to 6 minutes per side or to desired doneness. Remove the steaks to serving plates. Add the peppercorns to the sauté pan and whisk in the butter gradually. Pour the sauce over the steaks and serve.

Serves 6

Piquant Herb Sauce

½ cup fresh parsley sprigs
½ cup dry white wine
¼ cup white wine vinegar
1 small onion, quartered
2 large garlic cloves

½ teaspoon tarragon, crushed
¼ teaspoon chervil, crushed
⅛ teaspoon pepper
1 cup mayonnaise

Combine the parsley, wine, vinegar, onion, garlic, tarragon, chervil and pepper in a blender and process well at high speed. Pour into a saucepan. Cook over medium heat until reduced to ⅓ cup, stirring constantly. Strain through a wire mesh strainer and return to the saucepan. Stir in the mayonnaise and cook over medium heat until heated through. Garnish with chopped fresh parsley when ready to serve. Serve warm or chilled with beef tenderloin. This sauce can be made one day ahead. Chill, covered, until ready to serve.

Serves 10

Beef Stroganoff with Tomatoes

1 1/2 pounds top sirloin steak, halved lengthwise and
    cut into 1/4-inch strips
Salt and pepper to taste
2 tablespoons olive oil
1 tablespoon olive oil
1 large onion, thinly sliced
1 tablespoon olive oil
1 pound mushrooms, sliced
3 garlic cloves, chopped
1 teaspoon chopped fresh thyme, or
    1/4 teaspoon dried thyme
2 tablespoons all-purpose flour
1 (14-ounce) can diced tomatoes, drained
1/2 cup beef broth
Large pinch of cayenne pepper
Hot cooked egg noodles

Season the meat with salt and pepper. Heat 2 tablespoons olive oil in a large heavy
skillet over high heat. Add one-third of the meat and sauté for 2 minutes or just until
no longer pink. Remove the meat with a slotted spoon to a bowl. Repeat with the
remaining meat in 2 batches. Add 1 tablespoon olive oil to the skillet. Add the onion
and sauté over medium heat for 8 minutes or until golden brown. Remove the onion
with a slotted spoon and add to the meat. Add 1 tablespoon olive oil to the skillet.
Add the mushrooms, garlic and thyme and cook for 4 minutes or until the mushrooms
are tender, stirring occasionally. Sprinkle the flour over the mushrooms. Cook for
1 minute, stirring constantly. Add the meat, onion and accumulated juices to the skillet.
Stir in the tomatoes, broth and cayenne pepper. Bring to a boil and reduce the heat to
medium-low. Uncover and simmer for 5 minutes or until the meat is tender. Serve over
hot noodles and garnish with chopped fresh parsley.

Serves 4

Sweet-and-Sour Stew

2 tablespoons vegetable oil
1 1/2 pounds stew beef
1 cup water
1/2 cup ketchup
1/4 cup packed brown sugar
1 tablespoon Worcestershire sauce
1 cup frozen pearl onions
Baby carrots to taste
1 teaspoon salt
1/4 cup cornstarch
1/4 cup cold water
Hot cooked noodles

Heat the oil in a heavy saucepan. Add the meat and brown on all sides. Stir in 1 cup water, ketchup, brown sugar, Worcestershire sauce, onions, carrots and salt. Bring to a simmer and cook, covered, over low heat for 1 1/2 to 2 hours or until the meat is tender. Combine the cornstarch and 1/4 cup cold water in a bowl and mix well. Stir into the beef stew. Cook until thickened and bubbly, stirring constantly. Serve over hot noodles. This may be baked at 325 degrees instead of cooked on top of the stove.

Serves 4

Beef Bourguignon

8 ounces thick bacon, cut into pieces
3 pounds lean stew beef
1 onion, chopped (about 1 cup)
3 tablespoons all-purpose flour
3 cups burgundy or other hearty
   red wine
1 (8-ounce) can diced tomatoes
1 1/2 teaspoons salt
1/2 teaspoon freshly ground pepper
1/2 teaspoon thyme

Chicken broth or beef broth
3 to 4 carrots, cut into bite-size pieces
2 cups frozen pearl onions (optional)
2 tablespoons butter
8 to 16 ounces (or more) shiitake
   mushrooms or other wild
   mushrooms, sliced
1/4 cup chopped fresh parsley
Hot cooked rice, noodles or mashed
   potatoes

Cook the bacon in a Dutch oven or heavy ovenproof saucepan until crisp. Remove with a slotted spoon to paper towels to drain. Add the beef a few pieces at a time and sauté over medium-high heat until brown on all sides. Remove the meat with a slotted spoon to a bowl. Repeat with the remaining meat. Add the onion, browned meat and flour to the saucepan. Cook over high heat for several minutes, stirring constantly. Stir in the wine, tomatoes, salt, pepper and thyme and just enough broth to cover the ingredients. Bring to a boil and stir in the bacon. Bake, covered, at 250 degrees for 3 hours or until the meat is tender.

Add the carrots to a saucepan of boiling water and cook for 5 minutes or just until tender. Remove with a slotted spoon to a bowl. Return the water to a boil. Add the onions and cook until tender; drain. Melt the butter in a skillet. Add the mushrooms and sauté until tender. Stir the carrots, onions and mushrooms into the beef mixture. Bake for 10 minutes longer. Adjust the seasonings to taste. Stir in the parsley. Serve over rice.

Serves 12

 Wild mushrooms will provide more flavor than button mushrooms. If using portobello mushrooms, remove the dark gills before sautéing.

Old Family Recipe Sauerbraten

1 (3-pound) boneless chuck roast
1 large onion, sliced
1 lemon, sliced
Handful of raisins
2 tablespoons mixed pickling spice
1/3 cup vinegar
2/3 cup water
2 tablespoons all-purpose flour
2 tablespoons vegetable oil
2 cups water
30 gingersnap cookies, crushed
1 cup warm water
Salt to taste
Hot cooked noodles

Place the meat in a sealable plastic bag. Add the onion, lemon, raisins, pickling spice, vinegar and 2/3 cup water. Seal the bag and place in a baking dish. Marinate in the refrigerator for 4 to 5 days, turning the bag occasionally. Remove the meat and reserve the marinade. Wipe the meat dry with paper towels. Rub the flour over all sides of the meat. Heat the oil in a heavy saucepan. Add the meat and brown on all sides. Add the reserved marinade and 2 cups water. Simmer, covered, for 3 hours or until the meat is very tender. Remove the meat to a platter and cover loosely with foil. Strain the cooking liquid through a wire mesh strainer and return to the saucepan. Combine the gingersnaps with 1 cup warm water in a bowl and mix well. Whisk the gingersnap mixture into the saucepan. Add additional water if needed to thin the gravy. Season with salt. Slice the meat across the grain and add to the gravy. Cook until heated through. Serve over hot cooked curly wide noodles on a serving platter with cooked baby carrots arranged around the edge. Pour any extra gravy into a gravy boat.

If time allows, chill the meat for easier slicing. The meat may be cooked in a pressure cooker for 45 minutes instead of on top of the stove.

Serves 6

Apple-Spiced Brisket

1 (5-pound) beef brisket, chuck roast or rump roast
1 teaspoon salt
2¹/₂ cups apple juice
1 teaspoon ground cinnamon
1 teaspoon ginger
1 teaspoon nutmeg
1 apple, peeled, cored and chopped
2 tablespoons raisins and/or prunes and/or dried apricots

Line a large roasting pan with heavy-duty foil, leaving a 1¹/₂-inch collar around the edges. Prick the meat with a fork on both sides and sprinkle with the salt. Place on a rack in the prepared roasting pan. Bake, uncovered, at 450 degrees for 1 hour. Remove any excess fat from the pan. Combine the apple juice, cinnamon, ginger and nutmeg in a bowl and mix well. Pour over the meat. Cover the pan with heavy-duty foil and seal tightly. Bake at 350 degrees for 1¹/₂ hours or until the meat is tender. Remove the meat to a warm serving platter and keep warm in a low oven. Pour the meat juices into a saucepan. Stir in the apple and raisins. Bring to a boil and reduce the heat. Simmer for 3 minutes or until the apple is tender. Slice the meat across the grain and spoon the sauce over the meat.

Serves 10

Mexican Meat Loaf

2 eggs, beaten
1/2 cup taco sauce
2 to 3 jalapeño chiles, finely chopped
1/3 cup whole wheat bread crumbs
1 teaspoon salt
1/4 cup chopped onion
11/2 pounds ground beef
1/4 cup taco sauce
1/3 cup shredded Monterey Jack cheese

Combine the eggs, 1/2 cup taco sauce, the jalapeños, bread crumbs, salt and onion in a bowl and mix well. Add the ground beef and mix well. Shape the mixture into a 5×9-inch loaf. Place on a lightly greased rack in a broiler pan. Spread 1/4 cup taco sauce over the top. Bake at 325 degrees for 1 hour. Sprinkle with the cheese and bake for 5 minutes longer or until the cheese melts.

Serves 6

Balsamic-Marinated Pork Tenderloin

1 1/2 cups vegetable oil
3/4 cup soy sauce
2 tablespoons dry mustard
1 tablespoon pepper
1/3 cup lemon juice

1/2 cup balsamic vinegar
2 tablespoons finely chopped fresh
    parsley
1 garlic clove, minced
2 (1-pound) pork tenderloins

Whisk the oil, soy sauce, dry mustard, pepper, lemon juice, vinegar, parsley and garlic in a bowl. Place the tenderloins in a sealable plastic bag. Add the marinade and seal the bag. Marinate in the refrigerator for 24 hours, turning the bag occasionally. Remove the tenderloins and half the marinade to a roasting pan. Discard the remaining marinade. Bake at 350 degrees for 30 to 35 minutes or to 150 degrees on a meat thermometer.

Serves 4 to 6

Saté Babi (Grilled Pork Tenderloin Kabob)

1/2 cup vegetable oil
1/4 cup soy sauce
1/2 onion, sliced
3/4 teaspoon salt
Pepper to taste
1 tablespoon coriander
1 tablespoon cumin

1 tablespoon brown sugar
Dash of ginger
3 pounds pork tenderloin, cut into
    1 1/2-inch cubes
Fresh mushroom caps
Juice of 2 limes

Combine the oil, soy sauce, onion, salt, pepper, coriander, cumin, brown sugar and ginger in a bowl and mix well. Add the pork and stir to coat. Chill, covered, for 8 hours. Remove the pork and reserve the marinade. Thread the pork alternately with the mushroom caps onto long skewers. Grill for 15 to 20 minutes or until the pork is cooked through, turning often and basting occasionally with the marinade. Discard any remaining marinade. Sprinkle the lime juice over the pork and serve.

Serves 6

Marinated Pork Medallions

GINGER MAYONNAISE
2 cups mayonnaise
4$\frac{1}{2}$ teaspoons white wine vinegar
2 tablespoons finely chopped chives
$\frac{1}{2}$ to $\frac{3}{4}$ teaspoon ginger
$\frac{1}{4}$ teaspoon salt
Pinch of paprika

MEDALLIONS
$\frac{1}{2}$ cup olive oil
3 tablespoons white wine vinegar
3 tablespoons grated onion
$\frac{3}{4}$ teaspoon garlic powder
$\frac{1}{2}$ teaspoon salt
$\frac{1}{2}$ teaspoon chili powder
$\frac{1}{2}$ teaspoon oregano
3 (12-ounce) pork tenderloins
10 kaiser rolls (optional)

For the ginger mayonnaise, combine the mayonnaise, vinegar, chives, ginger, salt and paprika in a bowl and mix well. Chill, covered, until ready to serve.

For the medallions, combine the olive oil, vinegar, onion, garlic powder, salt, chili powder and oregano in a bowl and mix well. Place the pork tenderloins in a shallow dish. Pour the marinade over the tenderloins. Chill, covered, for 8 hours, turning occasionally. Remove the tenderloins and reserve the marinade. Place the tenderloins, fat side up, on a rack in a shallow roasting pan. Brush with the reserved marinade. Bake at 425 degrees for 10 minutes. Reduce the oven temperature to 350 degrees and bake for 25 minutes, basting occasionally with the marinade. Discard any remaining marinade. Slice the tenderloins and serve on the rolls with the ginger mayonnaise.

Serves 10

 Serve on small dinner rolls or Angel Biscuits (page 64) for a cocktail buffet.

Tangy Grilled Pork Tenderloin

1/2 cup teriyaki baste and glaze sauce
1/4 cup dry red wine
1/2 teaspoon red pepper flakes, or 1 teaspoon hot sesame oil
1 (2-pound) pork tenderloin

Combine the teriyaki sauce, wine and red pepper flakes in a measuring cup and mix well. Place the tenderloin in a sealable plastic bag. Pour the marinade over the tenderloin and seal the bag. Chill for 8 hours or overnight. Remove the tenderloin and reserve the marinade. Grill over medium-hot coals for 10 minutes per side or to 150 degrees on a meat thermometer, turning as needed and basting frequently with the marinade. Discard any remaining marinade. Let the tenderloin stand for 10 minutes before cutting into 1/2-inch-thick slices. Serve hot or cold.

Serves 6

Ginger Marinade

2 teaspoons grated fresh ginger
1/4 cup soy sauce
2 garlic cloves, minced
2 teaspoons sugar
4 teaspoons lemon juice
1/4 to 1/2 teaspoon red pepper flakes

Whisk the ginger, soy sauce, garlic, sugar, lemon juice and red pepper flakes in a bowl. Use to marinate pork, chicken or salmon in the refrigerator for 30 minutes. Bake or grill until cooked through. Bake in a baking bag with the marinade for an easy cooking method.

Makes 1/3 cup

Coffee- and Molasses-Brined Pork Chops

2 cups water
1½ cups strong brewed coffee, cooled
2 tablespoons salt
3 tablespoons brown sugar
2 tablespoons molasses
1 tablespoon Worcestershire sauce

4 (6-ounce) bone-in center cut or rib
  pork chops
1 cup wood chips
1 teaspoon freshly ground pepper
1 teaspoon each chili powder and cumin
1/4 teaspoon garlic salt

Mix the water, coffee, salt, brown sugar, molasses and Worcestershire sauce in a bowl until the sugar is dissolved. Place the pork chops in a sealable plastic bag; add the marinade and seal the bag. Chill for 1 to 3 hours. Soak the wood chips in water in a bowl for 1 hour; drain. Drain the pork chops, discarding the marinade. Pat dry with paper towels. Mix the pepper, chili powder, cumin and garlic salt in a small bowl. Rub over both sides of the pork chops. Place the wood chips over hot coals on the grill. Grill the pork chops until cooked through.

Serves 4

Brining

4 cups water
1/4 cup packed brown sugar
1/4 cup kosher salt, or 2 tablespoons
  table salt

Ice cubes
1 to 2 pounds poultry, pork
  or shrimp

Combine the water, brown sugar and salt in a baking dish. Stir until the sugar and salt are dissolved. Add a few ice cubes and stir until the ice is melted. Add the poultry, pork or shrimp and submerge in the brine. Cover and chill. Boneless chicken breasts and shrimp should be brined for 30 minutes. Bone-in chicken breasts, pork tenderloin and pork chops should be brined for 1 hour. A turkey requires a larger container and more brine and should be brined overnight. Rinse the poultry, pork or shrimp before cooking. Brining produces a juicier and more flavorful cooked product. The brine penetrates the proteins, helping them to absorb water and soften, which tenderizes the muscle.

Serves 4 to 6

Red Cabbage Pork Chops

4 (1-inch) boneless pork chops
Salt and pepper to taste
1 cup panko (Japanese bread crumbs)
1 tablespoon olive oil
1/4 cup thinly sliced onion
1 cup sliced cored peeled tart apple
1/4 cup sweetened dried cranberries (optional)
1 cup thinly sliced purple cabbage
1/4 cup apple brandy or apple juice concentrate

Season the pork chops with salt and pepper. Coat in the panko. Heat the olive oil in a skillet over medium-high heat. Add the pork chops and cook for 2 minutes per side or until brown. Cook for 4 minutes longer or until cooked through. Remove to an ovenproof plate and cover. Keep warm in a 225-degree oven. Add the onion to the skillet and sauté until tender, adding an additional small amount of olive oil if needed. Add the apple and dried cranberries and sauté until the apple is tender but not mushy. Remove the apple mixture to a bowl and keep warm. Add the cabbage and brandy to the skillet and stir to mix well. Cook, covered, until the cabbage is tender-crisp. Add the apple mixture to the skillet and toss well. Season with salt and pepper. Spoon the cabbage mixture onto a serving platter and top with the pork chops.

Serves 4

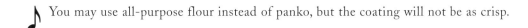 You may use all-purpose flour instead of panko, but the coating will not be as crisp.

Overnight Oven-Baked Pork Ribs

3 racks baby back ribs
1/2 cup pork rub seasoning or Memphis Rub (page 188)
Barbecue sauce

Rinse the ribs and pat dry with paper towels. Rub the seasoning generously on both sides of the ribs. Place the ribs on a rack in a 10×15-inch baking pan. Cover with foil, tenting the top, and seal the edges. Let stand at room temperature for 30 minutes. Bake the ribs at 225 degrees for 8 hours to overnight or until the meat is tender but not falling off the bones. Remove the foil and bake at 350 degrees for 15 minutes or until the ribs are beginning to crisp. Baste with barbecue sauce and bake for 15 minutes longer to caramelize.

Cut into individual ribs or 2 to 3 rib sections. Serve with barbecue sauce on the side. The ribs can be made ahead through the overnight baking. Chill, covered. When ready to serve, continue with crisping and caramelizing steps. The ribs can be frozen for up to two months. Thaw and reheat in the oven or microwave.

Serves 6

Penne in Cream Sauce with Sausage

1 tablespoon olive oil
1 tablespoon butter
1 onion, thinly sliced
3 garlic cloves, minced
1 pound sweet Italian sausage, casings removed
2/3 cup dry white wine
1 (14-ounce) can diced tomatoes
1 cup cream or heavy cream
1/4 cup chopped fresh flat-leaf parsley
Salt and pepper to taste
1 (16-ounce) package penne pasta,
    cooked al dente and drained
3/4 cup (3 ounces) freshly grated Parmesan cheese
2 tablespoons chopped fresh flat-leaf parsley
1/4 cup (1 ounce) freshly grated Parmesan cheese

Heat the olive oil and butter in a large heavy skillet over medium-high heat. Add the onion and garlic and sauté for 7 minutes or until tender and golden brown. Add the sausage and cook for 7 minutes or until brown and cooked through, stirring until crumbly; drain. Add the wine and boil for 2 minutes or until the liquid has almost evaporated. Stir in the undrained tomatoes and simmer for 3 minutes. Stir in the cream and simmer for 5 minutes or until slightly thickened. Stir in 1/4 cup parsley, salt and pepper. Place the hot cooked pasta in a large bowl. Add the cream sauce and 3/4 cup cheese and toss well to coat. Sprinkle with 2 tablespoons parsley and 1/4 cup cheese. The sauce can be made one day ahead. Chill, covered, until ready to use.

Serves 6

Rigatoni with Cheese and Italian Sausage

4 ounces Italian sausage, casings removed
2 garlic cloves, thinly sliced
1/2 cup prepared marinara sauce
1/2 teaspoon crushed red pepper
8 ounces rigatoni pasta, cooked al dente and drained
Salt and pepper to taste
1/4 cup (1 ounce) shredded mozzarella cheese
2 tablespoons grated Parmesan cheese
1 teaspoon chopped fresh flat-leaf parsley
Extra-virgin olive oil

Brown the sausage in a large heavy saucepan over medium-high heat, stirring until crumbly. Add the garlic and sauté for 2 minutes or until tender; drain. Stir in the marinara sauce and crushed red pepper. Stir in the pasta, salt and pepper and cook until heated through. Divide the pasta mixture evenly among four 1 1/4-cup soufflé dishes. Top each with equal portions of the mozzarella cheese and Parmesan cheese. Place under a broiler for 1 1/2 minutes or until the cheeses are melted and beginning to brown, watching closely to prevent burning. Sprinkle each with equal portions of the parsley and drizzle with olive oil.

Serves 4 as a first course or 2 as a main course

Italian Sausage and Wild Mushroom Risotto

2 tablespoons olive oil
1 pound sweet Italian sausage, casings removed and
    cut into 1/2-inch pieces
8 ounces portobello mushrooms, stemmed,
    dark gills removed and diced
10 ounces shiitake mushrooms, stemmed and diced
1 teaspoon chopped fresh thyme
1 teaspoon chopped fresh oregano
1/2 cup madeira
1/4 cup (1/2 stick) butter
1 large onion, chopped
4 garlic cloves, minced
2 cups arborio rice or other medium grain rice
    (about 13 ounces)
1 cup madeira
6 cups hot chicken stock or canned
    reduced-sodium chicken broth
Salt and pepper to taste
1 cup (4 ounces) freshly grated asiago cheese

Heat the olive oil in a large nonstick skillet over medium-high heat. Add the sausage
and sauté for 3 minutes or until beginning to brown; drain. Add the portobello
mushrooms, shiitake mushrooms, thyme and oregano and sauté for 10 minutes or until
the mushrooms are tender. Add 1/2 cup madeira and cook for 1 minute or until the
liquid has almost evaporated. Remove from the heat.

Melt the butter in a large heavy saucepan over medium-high heat. Add the onion and
garlic and sauté for 5 minutes or until tender. Add the rice and sauté for 2 minutes. Add
1 cup madeira and cook for 2 minutes or until the liquid has evaporated. Add 1 cup
of the hot stock and simmer until the stock is absorbed, stirring frequently. Continue
adding the stock, 1 cup at a time. Cook until the stock is absorbed before adding more,
stirring frequently. Cook for a total time of 25 minutes or until the rice is tender and
the mixture is creamy. Stir in the sausage mixture and cook until heated through. Season
with salt and pepper. Spoon into serving bowls and serve the cheese on the side.

Serves 8 as a first course or 4 as a main course

Grilled Marinated Lamb

4 teaspoons salt
4 teaspoons basil or oregano
4 teaspoons paprika
4 teaspoons Worcestershire sauce
2 tablespoons dry mustard
1/2 teaspoon (or less) pepper
1 cup cider vinegar
1/4 cup water
2 cups corn oil or canola oil
10 to 15 garlic cloves, cut into halves
1 (5-pound) leg of lamb, boned and butterflied

Combine the salt, basil, paprika, Worcestershire sauce, dry mustard, pepper, vinegar, water, corn oil and garlic in a bowl and mix well. Place the lamb in a 2-gallon sealable plastic bag. Pour the marinade over the lamb. Seal the bag and place in a large bowl or baking pan. Marinate in the refrigerator overnight. Bring the lamb to room temperature. Remove the lamb and discard the marinade. Grill the lamb over medium coals for 15 minutes per side or to desired doneness, turning several times. Remove the lamb to a serving platter and cover loosely with foil. Let stand for 20 to 30 minutes. Slice the lamb across the grain just before serving. You may add additional herbs such as rosemary to the marinade, if desired.

Serves 8 to 10

Grilled Glazed Lamb Chops

3/4 cup dry red wine
1/4 cup olive oil
3 tablespoons chopped fresh oregano
2 tablespoons minced garlic
2 teaspoons red wine vinegar
1/2 teaspoon salt
1/2 teaspoon pepper
8 (11/4-inch-thick) loin lamb chops
2 tablespoons honey

Combine the wine, olive oil, oregano, garlic, vinegar, salt and pepper in a large baking dish and mix well. Arrange the lamb chops in a single layer in the dish and turn to coat. Chill, covered, for at least 2 hours, turning and basting frequently. Remove the lamb chops to a plate. Stir the honey into the marinade. Grill the lamb chops over medium-high heat for 10 minutes for medium-rare or to desired doneness, turning and basting frequently with the marinade. Discard any remaining marinade.

Serves 8

 Honey promotes browning without adding sweetness.

Osso Buco

1 cup all-purpose flour
Salt and pepper to taste
6 veal shanks, cut crosswise 1¹/₂-inch thick
2 tablespoons olive oil
2 tablespoons butter
2 tablespoons olive oil
2 tablespoons butter
2 onions, diced (2 cups)
1 cup chicken broth
1 cup white wine
1 (14-ounce) can diced Italian tomatoes
1 teaspoon Kitchen Bouquet
¹/₂ teaspoon sweet basil
¹/₄ teaspoon oregano
¹/₂ teaspoon parsley flakes
1 teaspoon minced garlic
1 tablespoon brandy
¹/₄ cup (¹/₂ stick) chilled butter, cut into small pieces
    (optional)
Saffron rice or mashed potatoes

Place the flour in a paper bag and season with salt and pepper. Add the veal shanks, one at a time, and shake the bag to coat. Heat 2 tablespoons olive oil and 2 tablespoons butter in a Dutch oven or large heavy saucepan over medium-high heat. Add half the shanks and brown on all sides. Remove to a plate. Add 2 tablespoons olive oil and 2 tablespoons butter to the Dutch oven. Add the remaining shanks and brown on all sides. Remove to the plate. Add the onions to the Dutch oven and reduce the heat. Cook, covered, for 10 minutes or until tender. Stir in the broth, wine, tomatoes, Kitchen Bouquet, basil, oregano, parsley flakes, garlic and brandy. Arrange the veal shanks in a single layer on top. Simmer, covered, for 2 to 3 hours or until the veal is very tender, adding additional broth or wine if needed. For additional richness, whisk in butter pieces just before serving. Adjust the seasonings to taste. Serve over saffron rice or mashed potatoes. This may be made ahead. Chill, covered, for up to two days or freeze. Reheat slowly.

Serves 6

Veal and Mushroom Stew

1 to 2 tablespoons butter
2 pounds veal, cut into 1-inch cubes
2 tablespoons all-purpose flour
2 teaspoons sweet Hungarian paprika
1 1/2 teaspoons coriander
1/2 teaspoon salt, or to taste
1/4 teaspoon pepper, or to taste
3 cups canned plum tomatoes, drained, seeded and chopped
2 cups chicken broth
1 1/2 cups thinly sliced yellow onions
24 fresh or frozen pearl onions
2 garlic cloves, minced
1/4 cup chopped fresh flat-leaf parsley
1 tablespoon tarragon
Grated zest of 1 orange
1 tablespoon butter
12 ounces white mushrooms, cut into halves
3 tablespoons butter
3 tablespoons all-purpose flour
1/2 cup cream or heavy cream
Rice, noodles or mashed potatoes

Melt 1 to 2 tablespoons butter in a large heavy ovenproof saucepan over medium heat. Add the veal and sauté until the sides are no longer pink; do not brown. Combine 2 tablespoons flour, paprika, coriander, salt and pepper in a small bowl and mix well. Sprinkle over the veal. Cook for 5 minutes, stirring constantly. Stir in the tomatoes, broth, yellow onions, pearl onions, garlic, parsley, tarragon and orange zest. Bring to a boil. Bake, covered, at 350 degrees for 1 1/2 hours or until the veal is tender. Melt 1 tablespoon butter in a skillet over medium-high heat. Add the mushrooms and sauté until golden brown. Remove from the heat.

Strain the liquid from the stew through a wire mesh strainer into a bowl and reserve. Add 3 tablespoons butter to the saucepan and cook until melted. Add 3 tablespoons flour and cook for 3 minutes, whisking constantly. Whisk in the strained stew liquid gradually. Simmer for 5 minutes, stirring constantly. Stir in the cream. Adjust the seasonings to taste. Add the veal mixture and mushrooms. Simmer for 5 minutes, stirring occasionally. Serve over rice, noodles or mashed potatoes and garnish with chopped fresh parsley.

Serves 8

Beer Can Chicken

1 (4- to 5-pound) chicken
3 to 3¹/2 tablespoons Memphis Rub
(below)

1 (12-ounce) can beer

Rinse the chicken inside and out and pat dry with paper towels. Sprinkle 1 tablespoon Memphis Rub inside the body and neck cavities. Rub 1 tablespoon Memphis Rub all over the skin. Rub ¹/2 tablespoon of the Memphis Rub between the flesh and skin, if desired. Chill, covered, while preparing the grill. Set up the grill for indirect grilling, placing a drip pan in the center. Heat to medium. Open the beer can. Punch six or seven holes in the top of the can. Pour out one inch of beer. Spoon the remaining 1 tablespoon Memphis Rub into the beer. Hold the chicken upright and lower the chicken cavity over the beer can. Oil the grill rack. Stand the chicken upright on the center of the grill rack, using the beer can to form a tripod to support the chicken. Close the grill and cook for 2 hours or until very tender. Remove the chicken carefully to a work surface using tongs and a metal spatula under the beer can for support. Let stand upright for 5 minutes. Lift the chicken off the beer can and discard the beer can.

Serves 4 to 6

Memphis Rub

¹/4 cup paprika
1 tablespoon granulated sugar
1 tablespoon dark brown sugar
2 teaspoons salt
1 teaspoon freshly ground black pepper

1 to 3 teaspoons cayenne pepper
1 teaspoon dry mustard
1 teaspoon garlic powder
1 teaspoon onion powder
1 teaspoon celery salt

Combine the paprika, granulated sugar, brown sugar, salt, black pepper, cayenne pepper, dry mustard, garlic powder, onion powder and celery salt in a bowl and mix well. Store in a jar with a tight-fitting lid in a cool dark place for up to 6 months. Use on chicken or pork.

Makes about ¹/2 cup, enough for 4 racks of ribs

Brown Paper Bag Chicken

1 fryer chicken
Salt and pepper or favorite rub to taste
Brown paper grocery bag

Rinse the chicken inside and out and pat dry with paper towels. Season inside and out with salt and pepper. Place inside the paper bag and staple the bag closed. Place in a 10×15-inch baking pan. Bake at 400 degrees for 1 hour or until the chicken is cooked through. Remove carefully from the bag to a cutting board and carve. You may use chicken parts instead of a whole chicken.

Serves 2 to 4

Grilled Marinated Chicken

3/4 cup vegetable oil
1/3 cup soy sauce
3 tablespoons Worcestershire sauce
1/4 cup red wine vinegar
Juice of 1 lemon
1 tablespoon dry mustard
1 teaspoon salt
2 tablespoons finely chopped fresh parsley
1 garlic clove, crushed
2 pounds chicken pieces

Whisk the oil, soy sauce, Worcestershire sauce, vinegar, lemon juice, dry mustard, salt, parsley and garlic in a bowl. Place the chicken in a sealable plastic bag or glass baking dish. Pour the marinade over the chicken and seal the bag or cover the baking dish. Chill for 6 to 24 hours. Remove the chicken and discard the marinade. Grill the chicken until cooked through.

Serves 6

Moroccan Chicken

Sauce
1/4 cup reduced-sugar orange marmalade or
    apricot preserves
1 cup sour cream
1 teaspoon dry mustard
1/2 teaspoon cumin
1/4 teaspoon celery seeds
2 tablespoons finely chopped green onions

Chicken
1/2 teaspoon cinnamon
1 teaspoon salt
1/2 teaspoon pepper
3 to 31/2 pounds chicken pieces
1/4 cup reduced-sugar orange marmalade or
    apricot preserves

For the sauce, combine the marmalade, sour cream, dry mustard, cumin, celery seeds and green onions in a bowl and mix well.

For the chicken, combine the cinnamon, salt and pepper in a bowl and mix well. Rub evenly over the chicken pieces. Place the chicken, skin side down, on a rack in a broiler pan. Broil on the middle rack in the oven for 15 minutes. Turn the chicken and broil for 15 minutes or until cooked through and the skin is crisp. Brush the marmalade over the chicken and broil for 2 minutes longer. Serve with the sauce.

Serves 6

Catalan Chicken

    3 tablespoons olive oil
    1 (3-pound) chicken, cut up
    2 garlic cloves, chopped
    1 cup chicken broth
    1 cup pinot noir
    2 red bell peppers, roasted, peeled, seeded and sliced
    2 tomatoes, peeled and cut into wedges
    4 ounces oil-cured olives, pitted
    1/2 cinnamon stick
    Salt to taste
    Hot cooked rice

Heat the olive oil in a large deep skillet or Dutch oven. Add the chicken and brown on all sides. Add the garlic and sauté for a few minutes. Stir in the broth, wine, bell peppers, tomatoes, olives, cinnamon stick and salt. Simmer, covered, for 45 to 60 minutes or until the chicken is cooked through. Remove and discard the cinnamon stick. Serve over rice or with grilled bread.

Serves 4

♪ Pablo Casals, the great cellist, was born in Catalonia, a region of Spain.

Opulent Chicken

4 boneless skinless chicken breasts
Paprika to taste
Salt and pepper to taste
2 tablespoons butter
1 (15-ounce) can artichoke hearts, drained
2 tablespoons butter
8 ounces mushrooms, sliced or whole (if small)
1 teaspoon tarragon
3 tablespoons all-purpose flour
1/3 cup sherry
1 1/2 cups chicken broth

Sprinkle the chicken with paprika, salt and pepper. Melt 2 tablespoons butter in a skillet. Add the chicken and cook until golden brown on both sides. Remove to a baking dish. Spread the artichoke hearts over the chicken. Add 2 tablespoons butter to the skillet. Add the mushrooms and tarragon and sauté for 5 minutes. Sprinkle with the flour. Stir in the sherry and broth. Simmer for 5 minutes, stirring frequently. Pour evenly over the chicken and artichoke hearts. Bake, covered, at 375 degrees for 45 minutes or until the chicken is cooked through.

Serves 4

Oven-Baked Lime Chicken

1 tablespoon grated lime zest
2 tablespoons brown sugar
Juice of 2 to 4 limes (or more)
3¹/2 pounds chicken pieces or boneless chicken breasts
3 tablespoons butter
1/4 cup all-purpose flour
1¹/4 teaspoons salt
1/2 teaspoon pepper
1 (14-ounce) can chicken broth

Combine the lime zest and brown sugar in a small bowl and mix well. Sprinkle
2 tablespoons of the lime juice over the chicken and let stand for a few minutes.
Melt the butter in a 9×13-inch baking pan in the oven. Mix the flour, salt and pepper
together. Coat the chicken in the flour mixture and then place in the baking pan,
turning to coat with the melted butter. Arrange the chicken, skin side down, in the
baking pan. Sprinkle the lime zest mixture over the chicken. Pour the broth and any
remaining lime juice into the baking pan. Bake at 400 degrees for 50 minutes or until
the chicken is cooked through, basting occasionally with the pan juices. Use 1/2 can
of broth if cooking boneless chicken breasts.

Serves 6 to 8

Champagne Chicken

1/4 cup all-purpose flour
1 teaspoon salt
1/2 teaspoon pepper
4 boneless skinless chicken breasts, rinsed and patted dry
1/2 cup (1 stick) butter
1 pound mushrooms, sliced
1 cup cream or heavy cream
1/4 cup Champagne or white wine

Mix the flour, salt and pepper together. Coat the chicken in the flour mixture, shaking off any excess. Melt the butter in a skillet over medium heat. Add the chicken and lightly brown on both sides. Remove the chicken to a plate. Add the mushrooms and sauté for 5 minutes; drain. Stir in the cream and add the chicken. Simmer over low heat for 10 minutes or until the chicken is cooked through. Remove the chicken to a warm platter and keep warm. Add the Champagne to the skillet and bring to a boil. Cook until creamy, stirring constantly. Spoon the sauce over the chicken.

Serves 4

♪ To keep an open bottle of Champagne from going flat, place a spoon handle in the bottle neck and store in the refrigerator. It will stay bubbly for several days.

Rosemary Chicken

1 cup dry bread crumbs or panko
2 tablespoons chopped fresh rosemary
2 tablespoons grated Parmesan cheese
4 boneless skinless chicken breasts
1 to 2 tablespoons olive oil

Mix the bread crumbs, rosemary and cheese together. Coat the chicken in the bread crumb mixture. Heat the olive oil in a large skillet. Add the chicken and cook until brown on both sides and cooked through. The chicken may be cooked in a baking dish coated with the olive oil at 350 degrees until cooked through or may be grilled.

Serves 4

 Panko are Japanese bread crumbs that are coarser than bread crumbs normally used in the United States. Using panko results in a crunchier crust. Panko bread crumbs are found in the Asian section of the grocery store.

Walnut Chicken Stir-Fry

2 tablespoons light soy sauce
1 1/2 teaspoons cornstarch
1 tablespoon dry sherry
1 teaspoon grated fresh ginger, or 1/4 teaspoon ground ginger
1/2 teaspoon sugar or Splenda sweetener
1/4 teaspoon red pepper flakes
1 teaspoon vegetable oil
1/2 green bell pepper, sliced
1 onion, sliced
1/2 cup walnut halves or pieces
1 teaspoon vegetable oil
8 ounces boneless chicken breasts, cut into 1-inch pieces
1/2 cup (about) chicken broth
Hot cooked rice

Combine the soy sauce, cornstarch, sherry, ginger, sugar and red pepper flakes in a bowl and mix well. Heat 1 teaspoon oil in a nonstick 10-inch skillet over medium-high heat for 2 minutes. Add the bell pepper and onion and stir-fry for 2 minutes. Remove with a slotted spoon to a bowl. Add the walnuts to the skillet and stir-fry for 1 to 2 minutes. Remove to the bowl. Add 1 teaspoon oil to the skillet. Add the chicken and stir-fry until the chicken is cooked through. Stir in the soy sauce mixture and chicken broth. Cook until thickened, stirring constantly. Add the vegetables and walnuts. Cook for 1 minute or until heated through, stirring constantly. Serve over hot white or brown rice.

Serves 2

Stir-Fried Chicken and Broccoli with Black Bean Sauce

1 pound boneless chicken breasts, cut into 1/4-inch strips
1 tablespoon dry sherry
1 tablespoon teriyaki sauce or soy sauce
2 tablespoons cornstarch
1/4 cup water
2/3 cup chicken broth
2 tablespoons rice vinegar
1/4 cup soy sauce
2 tablespoons black bean sauce
1/2 teaspoon chili paste (optional)
2 teaspoons vegetable oil
1 teaspoon sesame oil
3 cups broccoli florets
1 cup red bell pepper strips
1 1/2 teaspoons minced fresh ginger
Hot cooked rice

Combine the chicken, sherry and teriyaki sauce in a bowl and mix well. Chill, covered, for 20 minutes. Combine the cornstarch and water in a bowl and stir until smooth. Stir in the broth, vinegar, soy sauce, black bean sauce and chili paste. Heat the vegetable oil and sesame oil in a wok or large nonstick skillet over medium-high heat. Add the chicken mixture and stir-fry for 3 minutes or until the chicken is cooked through. Remove the chicken with a slotted spoon to a bowl. Add the broccoli, bell pepper and ginger to the wok and stir-fry for 2 minutes. Add the broth mixture and chicken. Bring to a boil and cook just until the vegetables are tender-crisp, stirring occasionally. Serve over hot rice.

Serves 4

Irish Oatmeal Chicken

1/2 cup Irish oats (do not substitute)
4 chicken breasts, halved, boned and skinned
Buttermilk
Salt and pepper to taste
1/4 cup (1/2 stick) butter
2 tablespoons butter
2 tablespoons minced shallots
4 ounces cremini mushrooms or shiitake mushrooms, stemmed and sliced
1/2 cup white wine
1 cup cream or heavy cream

Grind the oats in a food processor to medium-fine and remove to a shallow dish. Place the chicken breasts in a bowl and cover with buttermilk. Let soak for 30 minutes. Remove the chicken and pat dry with paper towels. Discard the buttermilk. Season the chicken lightly with salt and pepper and coat in the oats. Melt 1/4 cup butter in a skillet over medium-high heat. Add the chicken and cook 3 minutes per side or until light brown. Reduce the heat and cook for 5 minutes per side or until cooked through. Remove to a platter. Cover and keep warm.

Heat 2 tablespoons butter in a saucepan until foamy. Reduce the heat and add shallots and mushrooms. Sauté until tender. Stir in the wine. Cook until the wine is reduced by half. Stir in the cream. Cook until the cream is reduced to about 3/4 cup. Spoon the sauce over the chicken.

Serves 4

♪ Irish oats, or steel-cut oats, have not been steamed or rolled as with old-fashioned oats. They have a chewy texture and take much longer to cook.

Curried Chicken with Mango Chutney

2 teaspoons canola oil
1 1/2 pounds boneless chicken breasts, cut into 2-inch pieces
1/2 teaspoon salt
1/4 teaspoon pepper
1 Granny Smith apple, peeled, cored and chopped
1 onion, chopped
1 teaspoon grated fresh ginger
1 garlic clove, minced
1 tablespoon curry powder
1/2 cup mango chutney
1/4 cup currants
1/4 cup low-sodium chicken broth
1/4 cup fat-free half-and-half
1 tablespoon chopped fresh parsley
2 tablespoons slivered almonds, toasted
Hot cooked white rice

Heat the canola oil in a large skillet. Add the chicken and sauté until the chicken is cooked through. Sprinkle with the salt and pepper. Remove with a slotted spoon to a bowl. Add the apple, onion, ginger and garlic to the drippings in the skillet. Sauté for 6 minutes or until tender. Stir in the curry powder, chutney, currants, broth, half-and-half, parsley and almonds to the skillet. Bring to a boil, stirring frequently. Add the chicken and reduce the heat. Simmer until the sauce thickens, stirring occasionally. Serve over hot rice.

Serves 6

Easy Paella

2 pounds (3 to 4) boneless skinless chicken breasts,
  cut into 3/4-inch pieces
2 tablespoons all-purpose flour
2 tablespoons olive oil
1 pound kielbasa or similar sausage, cut into 1/2-inch pieces
2 teaspoons paprika
1/2 teaspoon salt
1/4 teaspoon freshly ground pepper
1 onion, thinly sliced
1 tomato, diced
1 (2-ounce) jar sliced pimento
1 (14-ounce) can chicken broth
1 (10-ounce) package frozen green peas
1 cup converted rice
1 (5-ounce) package yellow rice
1 pound fresh large deveined peeled shrimp

Coat the chicken in the flour. Heat the olive oil in a large skillet. Add the chicken
and sauté until brown on all sides. Stir in the kielbasa, paprika, salt, pepper, onion,
tomato, pimento, broth and peas. Simmer for 10 minutes, stirring occasionally. Stir in
the converted rice, yellow rice and shrimp. Simmer, covered, for 15 minutes.

Serves 8 to 10

Baked Sesame Chicken Noodles

1 tablespoon dark sesame oil
1 cup red bell pepper strips
8 ounces shiitake mushrooms caps, sliced
    (or other mushrooms)
2 (6-ounce) boneless skinless chicken breasts,
    cut into 1/2-inch pieces
1 teaspoon minced fresh ginger
3 garlic cloves, minced
1/4 cup low-sodium soy sauce
1 tablespoon cornstarch
1 cup fat-free reduced-sodium chicken broth
2 tablespoons cream sherry
1 tablespoon rice vinegar
1/2 teaspoon crushed red pepper
8 ounces spaghetti or linguine pasta, broken in half,
    cooked al dente and drained
2 cups thinly sliced bok choy
3/4 cup sliced green onions
2 teaspoons sesame seeds
1 cup panko (Japanese bread crumbs)
2 tablespoons butter, melted
1 teaspoon sesame seeds

Heat the sesame oil in a large heavy saucepan over medium-high heat. Add the bell pepper and mushrooms and sauté for 2 minutes. Add the chicken, ginger and garlic and sauté for 3 minutes. Stir in the soy sauce. Cook for 2 minutes, stirring frequently. Whisk the cornstarch into the broth in a bowl. Add to the chicken mixture and cook for 2 minutes or until slightly thickened, stirring constantly.

Remove from the heat and stir in the sherry, vinegar and red pepper. Add the pasta, bok choy, green onions and 2 teaspoons sesame seeds and toss well. Spoon into an 8×8-inch baking dish lightly coated with nonstick cooking spray. Combine the panko, melted butter and 1 teaspoon sesame seeds in a bowl and mix well. Sprinkle evenly over the pasta mixture. Bake at 400 degrees for 20 minutes or until light brown.

Serves 4

Chicken and Crescent Amandine

3 cups chopped cooked chicken or turkey
1 (10-ounce) can condensed cream of chicken soup
1 (8-ounce) can water chestnuts, drained and sliced
1 (4-ounce) can mushroom pieces and stems, drained
2/3 cup mayonnaise
1/2 cup chopped celery
1/2 cup chopped onion
1/2 cup sour cream
1 (8-count) can refrigerator crescent rolls
1/2 cup slivered almonds
2/3 cup shredded Swiss cheese or American cheese
2 to 4 tablespoons margarine, melted

Combine the chicken, soup, water chestnuts, mushrooms, mayonnaise, celery, onion and sour cream in a large saucepan and mix well. Cook until hot and bubbly, stirring frequently. Pour into an ungreased 9×13-inch baking pan. Unroll the crescent dough on a work surface to form two rectangles and press the seams to seal. Place on top of the chicken mixture. Combine the almonds, cheese and melted margarine in a bowl and mix well. Spread evenly over the dough. Bake at 375 degrees for 20 to 25 minutes.

Serves 6 to 8

Almond Chicken Pie

1 tablespoon butter
2 cups sliced celery
1 tablespoon all-purpose flour
1¹/2 cups (6 ounces) shredded sharp Cheddar cheese
3 cups chopped cooked chicken or turkey
¹/4 cup slivered almonds, toasted
1 cup mayonnaise
1 tablespoon lemon juice
1 teaspoon oregano
¹/4 teaspoon salt
¹/4 teaspoon pepper
1 unbaked (9-inch) pie shell
¹/2 cup (2 ounces) shredded sharp Cheddar cheese
¹/4 cup slivered almonds, toasted

Melt the butter in a skillet. Add the celery and sauté until tender. Combine the flour and 1¹/2 cups cheese in a bowl and toss well. Add the celery, chicken, ¹/4 cup almonds, mayonnaise, lemon juice, oregano, salt and pepper and mix well. Spoon into the pie shell. Sprinkle with ¹/2 cup cheese and ¹/4 cup almonds. Bake at 400 degrees for 30 to 35 minutes.

This can be made ahead. Chill, covered, until ready to reheat and serve.

Serves 6

Baked Chicken Pasta

2 tablespoons olive oil
1 tablespoon minced garlic
2 cups sliced fresh mushrooms
1 cup diced onion
2 to 3 cups diced uncooked chicken breasts
12 ounces uncooked penne or fusilli pasta
2 (10-ounce) cans condensed golden mushroom soup
2 cups half-and-half
1/2 cup (2 ounces) grated Parmesan cheese
2 cups (8 ounces) shredded mozzarella cheese

Heat the olive oil in a large saucepan. Add the garlic, mushrooms and onion and sauté for 3 minutes. Add the chicken and sauté for 5 minutes. Add the pasta, soup, half-and-half and Parmesan cheese and mix well. Pour into a 9×13-inch baking dish. Bake, covered, at 350 degrees for 30 minutes. Sprinkle with the mozzarella cheese. Bake, uncovered, for 15 to 20 minutes longer.

This can be frozen after baking. To reheat, bring to room temperature and bake at 350 degrees for 30 to 45 minutes.

Serves 8

Southwestern Chicken and Black Bean Stew

2 thick slices bacon
1¼ pounds boneless chicken
   thighs, trimmed
Salt and pepper to taste
1 large yellow onion, diced
1 large garlic clove, minced
½ red bell pepper, diced
2 teaspoons chili powder
1 heaping teaspoon cumin

¾ cup beer
1 (15-ounce) can black beans, drained
   and rinsed
½ to 1 teaspoon chipotle sauce
1¾ cups chicken broth
1 lime
3 tablespoons chopped fresh cilantro
Hot cooked rice (optional)

Cook the bacon in a large heavy saucepan until slightly crisp; drain on paper towels and crumble. Drain most of the bacon drippings from the saucepan. Season the chicken with salt and pepper. Add half the chicken to the saucepan and sauté over medium heat for 2 to 3 minutes per side or until well browned. Remove to a plate. Repeat with the remaining chicken. Remove all but 1 tablespoon of the drippings from the pan (or remove all drippings and add a small amount of the broth) and add the onion, garlic and bell pepper. Sauté for 7 minutes or until the onion begins to caramelize. Increase the heat to high and add the chili powder and cumin. Cook for 30 seconds, stirring constantly. Stir in the beer and cook for 3 minutes or until almost all of the liquid has evaporated. Stir in the black beans, chipotle sauce and broth. Bring to a boil and reduce the heat. Simmer for 5 minutes.

Remove 2 cups of the mixture to a blender or food processor and purée. Return the puréed mixture to the saucepan. Add the chicken. Cook, partially covered, for 20 minutes or until the chicken is cooked through. Add more broth if the mixture seems too thick.

Juice half the lime and cut the remaining half into wedges. Add the lime juice, bacon and cilantro to the stew. Simmer for 5 minutes, stirring frequently. Adjust the seasonings to taste. Serve with the lime wedges and garnish with chopped fresh cilantro. Serve over hot rice.

Serves 4

Turkey Loaf with Creamy Horseradish Sauce

TURKEY
2 tablespoons canola oil
3 ribs celery, finely chopped
1 cup finely chopped onion
2 small carrots, finely chopped
3 garlic cloves, minced
1 teaspoon oregano
1 to 2 tablespoons chopped
   fresh rosemary
2 teaspoons salt
$1^{1}/2$ teaspoons pepper
2 pounds lean ground turkey
$1^{2}/3$ cups bread crumbs
2 eggs, beaten
$1/4$ cup heavy cream or milk

1 tablespoon finely chopped drained
   oil-pack sun-dried tomatoes
$1/2$ cup (2 ounces) freshly grated
   Parmesan cheese
$1/2$ cup (2 ounces) shredded
   mozzarella cheese
$1/2$ cup ketchup

SAUCE (OPTIONAL)
2 tablespoons butter
2 tablespoons all-purpose flour
$3/4$ cup cream or heavy cream
1 cup milk
$1/2$ teaspoon salt
$1/4$ teaspoon white pepper
1 tablespoon horseradish

For the turkey, heat the canola oil in a large skillet. Add the celery, onion, carrots and garlic and sauté for 5 minutes or until the vegetables are tender. Stir in the oregano, rosemary, salt and pepper. Cook for 2 minutes, stirring occasionally. Remove from the heat and let cool. Remove to a large bowl. Crumble the turkey and add to the vegetable mixture. Add the bread crumbs, eggs, cream, sun-dried tomatoes, Parmesan cheese, mozzarella cheese and ketchup and mix well. Pat into two loaf pans lined with waxed paper. Bake at 350 degrees for 1 hour or until cooked through. Let cool slightly before slicing.

For the sauce, melt the butter in a saucepan. Stir in the flour. Cook for 1 to 2 minutes, stirring constantly. Stir in the cream and milk. Cook until thickened, stirring constantly. Stir in the salt, pepper and horseradish. Serve with the turkey loaf.

Serves 8 to 12

Turkey and Wild Mushroom Loaf

2 tablespoons extra-virgin olive oil
3 cremini mushrooms, chopped
8 shiitake mushrooms, stemmed and chopped
1 shallot, chopped
Salt and pepper to taste
1 1/2 pounds ground turkey
3 to 4 sprigs fresh sage, chopped
   (about 2 tablespoons)
1 tablespoon Worcestershire sauce
3/4 cup Italian-style bread crumbs
1 egg, beaten
2 tablespoons butter
2 tablespoons all-purpose flour
3/4 cup chicken broth
1 teaspoon poultry seasoning

Heat a nonstick skillet over medium heat. Add the olive oil. Add the cremini mushrooms, shiitake mushrooms, shallot, salt and pepper. Sauté for 5 to 6 minutes or until the mushrooms are tender. Remove from the heat. Remove 1/4 cup mushrooms and set aside. Combine the remaining mushrooms, turkey, sage, Worcestershire sauce, bread crumbs and egg in a bowl and mix well. Form into a loaf and place in a greased small oval baking dish. Bake, covered, at 350 degrees for 30 minutes. Bake, uncovered, for 30 minutes longer or until cooked through.

Melt the butter in a saucepan. Whisk in the flour. Cook for 1 to 2 minutes, whisking frequently. Whisk in the broth and poultry seasoning. Season with salt and pepper. Simmer until thickened, whisking frequently. Stir in the reserved mushrooms. Serve over the meat loaf.

Serves 8

Roast Turkey with Prosciutto Hazelnut Crust

PROSCIUTTO BUTTER
1¹/₂ cups (3 sticks) unsalted butter,
    softened
6 tablespoons chopped hazelnuts
4¹/₂ teaspoons sherry wine vinegar
1 tablespoon chopped fresh thyme
2 teaspoons crushed black
    peppercorns
1 garlic clove, minced
³/₄ teaspoon salt
9 ounces thinly sliced prosciutto,
    chopped
3 green onions, chopped

GRAVY BASE
3 large shallots, finely chopped
1 cup dry white wine
1 bay leaf
1 large sprig fresh thyme
¹/₂ teaspoon chopped fresh rosemary
4 cups low-sodium chicken broth

TURKEY
1 (16- to 18-pound) whole turkey, or
    1 (6- to 7-pound) bone-in
    turkey breast
Salt and pepper to taste
1 onion, quartered
3 garlic cloves, cut into halves
5 large sprigs fresh thyme
5 large sage leaves
1 tablespoon crushed black
    peppercorns
5 cups (about) reduced-sodium
    chicken broth
¹/₄ cup all-purpose flour

For the prosciutto butter, combine the butter, hazelnuts, vinegar, thyme, peppercorns, garlic and salt in a bowl and mix well. Add the prosciutto and green onions and mix well.

For the gravy base, melt 2 tablespoons prosciutto butter in a heavy saucepan over medium-high heat. Add the shallots and sauté until golden brown. Stir in the wine, bay leaf, thyme and rosemary. Boil for 3 minutes or until the liquid is reduced to a glaze. Stir in the chicken broth. Bring to a boil and reduce the heat to medium-low. Simmer for 20 minutes. Remove and discard the bay leaf and thyme sprig.

For the turkey, rinse the turkey inside and out and pat dry with paper towels. Loosen the skin from the turkey. Reserve 1/4 cup prosciutto butter and set aside. Spread half of the remaining prosciutto butter under the skin of the turkey and spread the remaining prosciutto butter over the outside of the turkey. Season the outside of the turkey with salt and pepper and place on a rack in a large roasting pan. Place the onion, garlic, thyme sprigs, sage leaves and peppercorns in the turkey cavity (or under the breast if using a turkey breast). Tuck the wings tips under the bird and tie the legs together loosely. Roast on the bottom rack in the oven at 325 degrees for 1 1/2 hours. Add 2 cups of the broth to the pan and tent the turkey with foil. Roast for 2 hours longer or to 175 degrees on a meat thermometer inserted in the thickest part of the thigh, basting occasionally with the pan drippings and adding more broth, if needed. Remove the turkey to a platter and tent with foil. Let stand for 30 minutes.

Strain the pan juices through a wire mesh strainer into an 8-cup glass measuring cup. Remove the fat off the top. Stir in the gravy base and add enough of the remaining chicken broth to measure about 5 cups. Melt the reserved 1/4 cup prosciutto butter in a saucepan over medium-high heat. Whisk in the flour. Cook for 1 minute, whisking constantly. Add the pan juice mixture and bring to a boil. Boil for 5 minutes or until slightly thickened, whisking frequently. Season with salt and pepper. Serve with the turkey.

If using a turkey breast, use less prosciutto butter and gravy base. Roast the breast uncovered for 45 minutes. Add 2 cups of the broth to the pan and tent the turkey breast with foil. Roast for 1 hour and 15 minutes or to 160 degrees on a meat thermometer inserted in the thickest part of the breast, basting occasionally with the pan drippings.

The prosciutto butter and gravy base may be made one day ahead. Chill, covered, until ready to use. Bring the prosciutto butter to room temperature before using.

Serves 12 for a whole turkey, 6 for a turkey breast

Glazed Cornish Hens

1/4 cup whole cranberry sauce
2 tablespoons orange marmalade
1 tablespoon lemon juice
1 teaspoon finely chopped onion
1 teaspoon cornstarch
1/2 cup drained canned mandarin oranges
2 Cornish game hens
2 tablespoons butter, melted
Salt and pepper to taste

Combine the cranberry sauce, orange marmalade, lemon juice, onion and cornstarch in a saucepan. Cook over medium heat until bubbly, stirring constantly. Cook for 2 minutes longer or until thick, stirring constantly. Remove from the heat and stir in the oranges. Brush the game hens with the melted butter and season with salt and pepper. Place on a rack in a shallow roasting pan. Roast, covered with foil, at 375 degrees for 30 minutes. Roast, uncovered, 1 hour longer, basting with the orange sauce several times during the last 20 minutes of roasting. Reheat the remaining sauce and serve with the game hens. Serve with Wild Rice and Cranberry Pilaf (page 152).

Serves 2

Spicy Catfish with Bell Peppers and Onions

2 (6-ounce) catfish fillets
Salt and pepper to taste
All-purpose flour
2 tablespoons olive oil
1 1/2 teaspoons olive oil
1 onion, sliced
1/2 large red bell pepper, thinly sliced
1/2 large green bell pepper, thinly sliced
2 1/2 tablespoons white wine vinegar
1 tablespoon chopped drained canned pickled jalapeño chile
Salt and pepper to taste

Season the catfish with salt and pepper and dust with flour. Heat 2 tablespoons olive oil in a heavy skillet over medium-high heat. Add the catfish and cook for 4 minutes per side or until golden brown and the fish flakes easily. Remove the catfish to a serving plate and keep warm. Add 1 1/2 teaspoons olive oil to the skillet. Add the onion, red bell pepper and green bell pepper and sauté for 4 minutes or until the vegetables are tender-crisp. Add the vinegar and jalapeño and sauté for 1 minute. Season with salt and pepper. Spoon over the catfish. Serve with Mexican rice. Recipe can easily be doubled.

Serves 2

Lemon Soy-Baked Flounder Fillets

2 (6-ounce) flounder fillets or other mild fish
1 garlic clove, minced
2 tablespoons fresh lemon juice
2 teaspoons soy sauce
1/2 teaspoon sugar
1/2 teaspoon salt
2 tablespoons olive oil

Arrange the fish in a single layer in a glass or ceramic baking dish. Mix the garlic, lemon juice, soy sauce, sugar and salt in a small bowl. Whisk in the olive oil until emulsified. Pour evenly over the fish. Bake on the middle rack in the oven at 450 degrees for 5 to 7 minutes or until the fish flakes easily.

Serves 2

Grilled Red Snapper with Peach Salsa

2 tablespoons olive oil
1 1/2 teaspoons grated lemon zest or lime zest
3 tablespoons lemon juice or lime juice
1/4 teaspoon cumin
4 (4- to 6-ounce) red snapper fillets
Freshly ground pepper to taste
2 fresh peaches, peeled and diced
1/3 cup chopped fresh cilantro
2 tablespoons finely chopped sweet onion
Salt to taste

Whisk the olive oil, lemon zest, lemon juice and cumin in a bowl. Remove and reserve half the mixture to a bowl. Brush the remaining mixture over the fish. Sprinkle with pepper. Let stand for 20 minutes. Add the peaches, cilantro, onion, salt and pepper to the reserved lemon juice mixture; toss well. Grill the fish until it flakes easily. Serve topped with the peach salsa.

Serves 4

Poached Salmon with Lemon Garlic Mayonnaise

SALMON
4 (8-ounce) salmon fillets
1 cup dry white wine
1 cup water
2 teaspoons dill weed

LEMON GARLIC MAYONNAISE
1/2 cup mayonnaise
2 garlic cloves, minced
2 teaspoons fresh lemon juice
1 teaspoon Dijon mustard
1/2 teaspoon white pepper

For the salmon, place the salmon fillets in a 9×13-inch baking dish. Pour the wine and water over the fillets and sprinkle with the dill weed. Bake, covered with foil, at 350 degrees for 20 minutes or until the fish flakes easily.

For the garlic mayonnaise, combine the mayonnaise, garlic, lemon juice, Dijon mustard and pepper in a bowl and mix well. Arrange the salmon on a platter and top with the garlic mayonnaise or Lemon Basil Dip (page 35).

Serves 4

Mahogany Glazed Salmon

1/2 cup plain yogurt
2 tablespoons soy sauce
1 tablespoon olive oil
1 tablespoon minced fresh ginger
1 tablespoon lemon juice
Pinch of pepper
4 (6-ounce) salmon fillets
1 1/2 teaspoons chopped fresh chives

Combine the yogurt, soy sauce, olive oil, ginger, lemon juice and pepper in a shallow dish and mix well. Lay the salmon on top and turn to coat. Let stand, covered, for 20 to 30 minutes. Remove the salmon to a rack on a broiler pan. Broil 3 inches from the heat source for 4 to 5 minutes or until the fish flakes easily. Remove to warm serving plates and sprinkle with the chives. You may grill the salmon instead of broiling and may also use a whole salmon fillet instead of 4 salmon fillets.

Serves 4

Tilapia Parmesan

1/2 cup grated Parmesan cheese
1/4 cup (1/2 stick) butter, softened
3 tablespoons mayonnaise
3 tablespoons finely chopped green onions
1/4 teaspoon Old Bay seasoning
1/4 teaspoon basil
Pepper to taste
Hot red pepper sauce (optional)
2 pounds tilapia fillets
2 tablespoons lemon juice

Combine the cheese, butter, mayonnaise, green onions, Old Bay seasoning, basil, pepper and hot sauce in a bowl and mix well. Place the tilapia fillets in a 9×13-inch baking dish. Brush with the lemon juice. Bake at 350 degrees for 10 minutes or just until the fish is beginning to flake. Spread the cheese mixture over the fish. Bake for 5 minutes longer. Place under the broiler for 3 to 4 minutes or until golden brown.

Serves 4 to 6

Grilled Ahi Tuna

Sashimi-grade tuna steaks
Extra-virgin olive oil
Black sesame seeds
Kosher salt
Freshly ground pepper

Rub both sides of the tuna with olive oil and sprinkle with sesame seeds, salt and pepper. Grill over a very hot fire on a closed grill for 1 1/2 to 1 3/4 minutes per side; the tuna should be rare or very pink. Slice thinly across the grain and drizzle with teriyaki sauce and garnish with chopped green onions. You may cook the tuna in a cast-iron skillet lightly coated with olive oil over high heat instead of on a grill. Cook 2 minutes per side for rare.

Serves 1 tuna steak per person

Tuna Tapenade

4 cups (about) fresh spinach, steamed
1 large tomato, sliced
1 tablespoon olive oil
1 tablespoon butter
2 medium pieces tuna steak
1 tablespoon prepared basil pesto
2 tablespoons Black Olive Tapenade (page 33)

Divide the spinach between two serving plates and top with the tomato slices. Heat the olive oil and butter in a skillet over high heat. Add the tuna and cook for 2 minutes per side. Place the tuna over the tomato. Garnish each plate with half the pesto and half the tapenade. Serve with melon, other fresh fruit or Fruit Salsa (page 161).

Grilled Marinated Fillet of Tuna

2 cups teriyaki sauce
1/2 cup dry sherry
1/4 cup minced fresh ginger
1/2 cup finely chopped scallions
2 garlic cloves, thinly sliced
1/2 teaspoon cayenne pepper
2 teaspoons freshly ground black pepper
Juice of 2 lemons
4 (8- to 10-ounce) yellowfin tuna steaks, cut into 3-inch cubes
2 tablespoons olive oil
1/4 cup Japanese pickled ginger

Combine the teriyaki sauce, sherry, fresh ginger, scallions, garlic, cayenne pepper, black pepper and lemon juice in a large bowl and mix well. Add the tuna and stir to coat. Chill, covered, for 3 hours, turning the tuna every hour. Remove the tuna to a large plate and let stand for 30 minutes. Discard the marinade. Brush the tuna with the olive oil. Grill over a very hot fire for 1 to 2 minutes per side or until the outside is charred and the center is barely warm. Top each steak with equal amounts of the pickled ginger and serve.

Serves 4

Tuna with Lime and Spices

AVOCADO RELISH
1 small avocado, chopped
1 tablespoon lime juice
1 tablespoon finely chopped fresh cilantro
1 small red onion, finely chopped
1 fresh mango or tomato, chopped
Salt and pepper to taste

TUNA
$1/2$ teaspoon grated lime zest
1 garlic clove, crushed
2 teaspoons olive oil
1 teaspoon cumin
1 teaspoon coriander
Pepper to taste
4 (6-ounce) tuna steaks, rinsed and patted dry
1 tablespoon lime juice
Chopped fresh cilantro

For the relish, combine the avocado, lime juice, cilantro, onion, mango, salt and pepper in a bowl and mix well. Cover tightly and let stand at room temperature.

For the tuna, combine the lime zest, garlic, olive oil, cumin, coriander and pepper in a bowl and mix to a paste. Spread thinly over both sides of the tuna steaks. Heat a skillet over medium-high heat until hot. Add the tuna and press into the pan. Reduce the heat and cook for 5 minutes per side or until cooked through. Remove to paper towels to drain. Place the tuna on warm serving plates and sprinkle with the lime juice and cilantro. Serve with the avocado relish.

Serves 4

Whatcha Got? Fish Stew

AROMATICS
1 small onion, finely chopped
1 rib celery, finely chopped
1 stalk fennel, finely chopped
2 to 3 garlic cloves, finely chopped
1 (1-inch) piece fresh ginger, minced

SEASONING STYLES
Mediterranean — 1/4 teaspoon thyme plus 1 teaspoon oregano
Indian — Curry powder to taste
Northeastern — 1/2 cup clam juice plus pepper to taste
Southwestern — 1/2 teaspoon cumin, 1 teaspoon chili powder plus
    1 dried chipotle chile, chopped
Unusual — Fresh rosemary to taste plus 1/2 teaspoon anise seeds

FISH
1 pound shark steak, cut into small chunks
2 tilapia fillets plus 1 mahimahi fillet, cut into small chunks
1 cod fillet plus 1 catfish fillet, cut into small chunks
2 tablespoons olive oil
1 sweet potato, peeled and diced
3 carrots, peeled and diced
1 (12-ounce) can whole tomatoes, chopped
1 teaspoon paprika
Salt to taste
1 yellow summer squash, sliced crosswise (optional)
1/2 cup corn kernels (optional)
1/2 cup green peas (optional)

Select 1 or 2 aromatics, 1 seasoning style and 1 fish choice and set aside. Heat the
olive oil in a large skillet. Add the aromatics and sauté briefly. Add the sweet potato
and carrots and sauté for 1 minute. Stir in the tomatoes, paprika, salt and seasoning
style. Reduce the heat and simmer for 2 to 3 minutes. Add a small amount of water if
the mixture seems too thick. Stir in the fish, squash, corn and peas. Simmer, covered,
just until the fish flakes easily. Serve with lemon wedges, chopped fresh parsley,
chopped fresh cilantro, oyster crackers or tortilla chips.

Serves 6 to 8

Linguini and Clam Sauce

2 tablespoons olive oil
2 tablespoons butter
1 to 2 garlic cloves, finely chopped
1 (6-ounce) can minced clams, drained and liquid reserved
1/8 teaspoon oregano
Salt and pepper to taste
2 tablespoons chopped fresh parsley
4 to 5 ounces linguini pasta
Grated Parmesan cheese

Heat the olive oil and butter in a skillet. Add the garlic and sauté until light brown. Remove the garlic with a slotted spoon and discard. Pour the reserved clam liquid carefully into the skillet. Stir in the oregano, salt and pepper. Bring to a boil and reduce the heat. Simmer for 3 minutes. Stir in the clams and cook until heated through. Stir in the parsley. Cook the pasta in a saucepan of boiling water until al dente. Drain and return to the saucepan. Add the clam mixture and toss well to coat. Serve with generous amounts of cheese.

Serves 2

Pawleys Island Inn Crab Cakes

5 slices firm white sandwich bread
1 egg white, lightly beaten
1/2 cup mayonnaise
1/4 teaspoon cayenne pepper
1/4 teaspoon ground celery seeds
1/2 teaspoon dry mustard
Juice of 1/4 lemon
1 pound fresh lump crab meat or
    high-quality pasteurized crab meat
1/2 cup (1 stick) butter

Process the bread in a food processor to make crumbs. Remove 1 cup of bread crumbs to a bowl. Add the egg white, mayonnaise, cayenne pepper, celery seeds, dry mustard and lemon juice and mix well. Fold in the crab meat. Form into 8 patties, each about 1/3 cup. Spread the remaining bread crumbs over a plate. Coat the patties in the bread crumbs and place on a plate. Chill, loosely covered, for 1 to 4 hours. Melt half the butter in a large nonstick skillet over medium heat until hot but not smoking. Add half the crab cakes and fry for 4 minutes per side or until golden brown. Remove to paper towels to drain. Repeat with the remaining butter and crab cakes.

Serves 4

Lemon Scallops

1 1/2 pounds sea scallops
1/2 teaspoon salt
1/4 teaspoon pepper
2 teaspoons olive oil
2 teaspoons butter
3 tablespoons minced shallots
1/2 teaspoon minced garlic
1/2 cup dry white wine
2 tablespoons fresh lemon juice
2 tablespoons finely chopped fresh parsley

Sprinkle the scallops with the salt and pepper. Heat the olive oil in a skillet over medium-high heat. Add the scallops and cook for 2 minutes per side or until tender. Remove the scallops to a plate and keep warm. Add the butter to the skillet and cook until melted. Add the shallots and garlic and sauté for 30 seconds. Stir in the wine and lemon juice and cook for 1 minute longer. Add the scallops and toss to coat well. Remove from the heat and sprinkle with the parsley. Serve with lemon wedges.

Serves 4

Shrimp Baked with Feta Cheese

3 cups chopped fresh tomatoes, or 1 (28-ounce) can diced tomatoes
1/4 cup olive oil
1 teaspoon minced garlic
1/4 cup bottled clam juice
3/4 teaspoon oregano
1/2 teaspoon red pepper flakes, or to taste
2 tablespoons drained capers
Salt and freshly ground pepper to taste
3 tablespoons butter
1 pound large (26- to 30-count) deveined peeled shrimp
4 ounces crumbled feta cheese

Cook the tomatoes in a saucepan over medium-high heat until reduced to 2 cups, stirring frequently. Heat the olive oil in a saucepan. Add the tomatoes, garlic, clam juice, oregano, red pepper flakes, capers, salt and pepper. Bring to a simmer, stirring occasionally. Melt the butter in a skillet over medium-high heat. Add the shrimp and cook for 30 seconds per side or just until beginning to turn pink. Spoon equal portions of half the tomato mixture into 4 individual baking dishes. Top each with equal portions of the shrimp and butter mixture. Spoon the remaining tomato mixture equally over the shrimp. Top with equal portions of the cheese. Bake at 350 degrees for 10 to 15 minutes or until hot and bubbly. Serve with French bread to soak up the sauce.

Serves 4

Baked Chipotle Shrimp

1/2 cup (1 stick) butter
1/4 cup dry white wine
41/2 teaspoons Worcestershire sauce
1 to 2 canned chipotle chiles in adobo sauce, finely chopped
2 to 3 teaspoons adobo sauce
1 large garlic clove, minced
11/2 teaspoons salt
11/2 pounds fresh unpeeled shrimp

Melt the butter in a saucepan. Stir in the wine, Worcestershire sauce, chipotle chiles, adobo sauce, garlic and salt. Add the shrimp and toss well. Spread the mixture over the bottom of a large shallow roasting pan. Bake on the center rack of the oven at 400 degrees for 10 to 12 minutes or until the shrimp turn pink. Serve with a tossed green salad, crusty bread and plenty of napkins and damp paper towels to clean hands.

Serves 4

Artichoke Shrimp Casserole

1 (14-ounce) can artichoke hearts, drained, or
   1 package frozen artichoke hearts, thawed
12 ounces peeled cooked shrimp
2 tablespoons butter
4 ounces mushrooms, sliced
2 tablespoons butter
2 tablespoons all-purpose flour
1 1/2 cups milk
1 teaspoon Worcestershire sauce
1/4 cup dry sherry
Salt and pepper to taste
1/4 cup (1 ounce) grated Parmesan cheese
Dash of paprika

Cut the artichoke hearts into quarters and arrange in a buttered 9-inch baking dish. Top with the shrimp. Melt 2 tablespoons butter in a skillet. Add the mushrooms and sauté for 6 minutes. Pour evenly over the shrimp.

Melt 2 tablespoons butter in a saucepan over medium heat. Whisk in the flour. Cook until the flour is bubbly, whisking constantly. Whisk in the milk slowly. Cook until thickened, stirring constantly. Remove from the heat and stir in the Worcestershire sauce, sherry, salt and pepper. Adjust the seasonings to taste. Pour evenly over the shrimp mixture. Sprinkle with the cheese and paprika. Bake at 375 degrees for 20 minutes. Garnish with chopped fresh parsley.

This can be made ahead. Chill, covered, until ready to bake. Let stand at room temperature for 30 minutes before baking.

Serves 4

Shrimp and Crawfish Étouffée

1/2 cup (1 stick) butter
1 to 2 onions, chopped
1 green bell pepper, chopped
2 ribs celery, chopped
1/2 garlic bulb, peeled and cloves crushed
2 (8-ounce) cans tomato sauce
1 (10-ounce) can condensed golden mushroom soup
1 (10-ounce) can tomatoes with green chiles
3 cups water
1/2 to 1 teaspoon Creole seasoning
2 pounds fresh peeled shrimp and/or fresh peeled crawfish tails
1/2 cup chopped green onion tops
2 tablespoons chopped fresh parsley
Hot cooked rice

Melt the butter in a large saucepan. Add the onions, bell pepper, celery and garlic and sauté until the vegetables are tender. Stir in the tomato sauce, soup, tomatoes with green chiles, water and Creole seasoning. Simmer over low heat for 11/2 to 2 hours, stirring occasionally. Stir in the shrimp and/or crawfish, green onions and parsley. Simmer for 10 minutes or until the seafood is cooked through. Serve over hot rice.

Serves 4 to 6

Shrimp and Creamy Grits

3 cups water
1 cup cream or heavy cream
1/4 cup (1/2 stick) butter
1 teaspoon salt
1 cup stone-ground grits
1 1/2 pounds deveined peeled cooked shrimp,
   at room temperature
1 cup (4 ounces) finely shredded extra-sharp Cheddar cheese
2 garlic cloves, minced, or to taste

Bring the water, cream, butter and salt to a boil in a large saucepan over medium-high heat. Reduce the heat to low and whisk in the grits. Simmer, covered, for 15 to 20 minutes or until the grits are tender and creamy, stirring occasionally. Stir in the shrimp, cheese and garlic. Cook for 1 to 2 minutes or until heated through, stirring occasionally. Garnish with finely chopped chives or green onions. You may sauté the shrimp in butter and serve on top of the grits instead of adding to the grits.

Serves 6

Jambalaya

BASIC JAMBALAYA
3 tablespoons vegetable oil
1 1/2 pounds smoked sausage, cut into
  1/2-inch pieces
8 ribs celery, cut into 1/2 inch pieces
2 1/2 green bell peppers, cut into 1/2-
  inch pieces
3 onions, cut into 1/2-inch pieces
1 1/2 teaspoons garlic powder
1 1/2 teaspoons thyme
1/2 teaspoon cayenne pepper
1/2 teaspoon salt
4 bay leaves
3 (28-ounce) cans diced tomatoes
4 cups (or more) hot cooked rice

SHRIMP VERSION
1 teaspoon garlic powder
1 teaspoon salt
1/2 teaspoon black pepper
1/2 teaspoon cayenne pepper
1 1/2 pounds fresh deveined peeled
  shrimp
2 tablespoons vegetable oil
6 tablespoons chopped green onions
1 teaspoon fish sauce

CHICKEN VERSION
1/2 teaspoon salt
1/2 teaspoon black pepper
1/2 teaspoon cayenne pepper
1/2 teaspoon garlic powder
1 1/2 pounds boneless chicken pieces
3 tablespoons vegetable oil

Heat 3 tablespoons oil in a large saucepan over medium heat. Add the sausage and sauté for 3 to 4 minutes or until brown. Reduce the heat and stir in the celery, bell peppers and onions. Stir in the garlic powder, thyme, cayenne pepper, salt, bay leaves and tomatoes. Simmer, covered, for 25 to 30 minutes or until the vegetables are almost tender, stirring occasionally.

For the shrimp version, mix the garlic powder, salt, black pepper and cayenne pepper in a bowl. Add the shrimp and toss well to coat. Heat the oil in a skillet. Add the green onions and sauté until tender. Add the fish sauce and shrimp and sauté until the shrimp turn pink. Add to the sausage mixture. Cook until heated through, stirring occasionally. Remove and discard the bay leaves. Serve over the hot rice.

For the chicken version, mix the salt, black pepper, cayenne pepper and garlic powder in a bowl. Add the chicken and toss well to coat. Chill, covered, for 1 hour. Heat the oil in a skillet. Add the chicken and sauté until the chicken is cooked through. Add to the sausage mixture. Cook until heated through, stirring occasionally. Remove and discard the bay leaves. Serve over the hot rice. The basic jambalaya mixture may be made one day ahead. Chill, covered, overnight. Bring to a simmer and combine with the shrimp version or chicken version when ready to serve.

Serves 6 to 8

Shrimp Lasagna

2 eggs
1 cup evaporated milk
1 cup plain yogurt (do not use low-fat)
2 teaspoons minced garlic (about 4 cloves)
1 teaspoon basil
1 teaspoon oregano
1¹/₂ cups (6 ounces) shredded Swiss cheese
8 ounces crumbled feta cheese
¹/₃ cup chopped fresh parsley, or
   3 tablespoons dried parsley flakes
12 ounces angel hair pasta, cooked al dente and drained
1 (16-ounce) jar mild chunky salsa
1 pound deveined peeled cooked shrimp
2 cups (8 ounces) shredded mozzarella cheese

Combine the eggs, evaporated milk, yogurt, garlic, basil, oregano, Swiss cheese, feta cheese and parsley in a bowl and mix well. Spread half the pasta over the bottom of a 9×13-inch baking dish coated with nonstick cooking spray. Spread the salsa over the pasta. Top with half the shrimp and the remaining pasta. Top with the remaining shrimp. Pour the egg mixture evenly over the top and sprinkle with the mozzarella cheese. Bake at 350 degrees for 30 to 40 minutes or until bubbly and light brown. This can be made ahead. Chill, covered, until ready to serve. Reheat in the microwave.

Serves 8

Encores

Desserts

Music Education

The Guild provides volunteer and financial assistance for the Orchestra's fall middle school concerts for Guilford County seventh graders, as well as for elementary school concerts in the spring. Seventh grade students are invited to participate in a Guild-sponsored essay contest, meant to help them record their impressions of the symphonic experience.

In 2005, the Guild for the first time sponsored an art contest for Guilford County third and fourth graders, who attended the Greensboro Symphony Orchestra's Elementary School Concerts in the spring. This project invited students to "Listen, Imagine, and Draw" after the concert experience and involved collaboration with school personnel and GSO staff. Illustrating the Orchestra's and Guild's efforts on behalf of music education, representative drawings were featured in a display at the May 2005 masterworks concert.

This drawing by Austine Twyman, a third grade student in 2005 at Brooks Global Studies Extended-Year Magnet School, captures the conductor's energy and movement.

Fresh Apple Cake

3 cups all-purpose flour
1 teaspoon baking soda
1/2 teaspoon salt
1 teaspoon ground cinnamon
1/2 teaspoon nutmeg
11/2 cups vegetable oil

2 cups sugar
3 eggs
2 teaspoons vanilla extract
3 cups diced cored peeled apples
1 cup chopped pecans

Sift the flour, baking soda, salt, cinnamon and nutmeg together. Beat the oil, sugar and eggs in a large bowl until creamy. Stir in the dry ingredients. Stir in the vanilla, apples and pecans. Pour into a greased and floured 9- or 10-inch tube pan. Bake at 350 degrees for 1 hour and 15 minutes or until a wooden pick inserted in the center comes out clean. Cool in the pan for 10 minutes. Invert onto a serving plate and cool completely. Serve plain or frost the top and sides with Cream Cheese Frosting (below) or drizzle with Caramel Icing (below).

Serves 12 to 16

Cream Cheese Frosting

8 ounces cream cheese, softened
2 tablespoons butter, softened
1 teaspoon vanilla extract

1 (16-ounce) package
   confectioners' sugar

Beat the cream cheese and butter in a bowl until light and fluffy. Beat in the vanilla and confectioners' sugar until smooth.

Caramel Icing

1/2 cup evaporated milk
11/2 cups packed brown sugar

1/4 cup (1/2 stick) butter

Combine the evaporated milk, brown sugar and butter in a heavy saucepan. Cook to 234 degrees, soft-ball stage, stirring constantly. Remove from the heat and let cool slightly.

Blackberry Lemon Pudding Cake

1/4 cup all-purpose flour
2/3 cup granulated sugar
1/8 teaspoon salt
1/8 teaspoon nutmeg
1 cup low-fat buttermilk
1 teaspoon grated lemon zest
1/4 cup fresh lemon juice
2 tablespoons butter, melted
2 egg yolks
3 egg whites
1/4 cup granulated sugar
1 1/2 cups blackberries, or 2 cups blueberries
Confectioners' sugar

Combine the flour, 2/3 cup granulated sugar, salt and nutmeg in a bowl and mix well. Add the buttermilk, lemon zest, lemon juice, butter and egg yolks and whisk until smooth. Beat the egg whites in a bowl with an electric mixer at high speed until foamy. Beat in 1/4 cup granulated sugar, 1 tablespoon at a time and beat until stiff. Fold one-fourth of the egg whites into the lemon mixture. Fold in the remaining egg whites gently. Fold in the blackberries. Pour into an 8×8-inch baking pan coated with nonstick cooking spray. Place the baking pan in a larger baking pan. Add enough hot water to the larger pan to come 1 inch up the sides of the smaller pan. Bake at 350 degrees for 35 minutes or until the center springs back when lightly touched. Remove the smaller pan to a wire rack. Dust with confectioners' sugar. Serve warm or at room temperature.

Serves 5

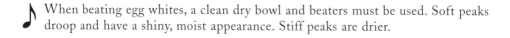 When beating egg whites, a clean dry bowl and beaters must be used. Soft peaks droop and have a shiny, moist appearance. Stiff peaks are drier.

1-2-3-4 Pound Cake

3 cups all-purpose flour
2 teaspoons baking powder
Pinch of salt
1 cup (2 sticks) butter, softened
2 cups sugar
4 eggs
1 cup milk
1 teaspoon vanilla extract
1 teaspoon almond extract

Sift the flour, baking powder and salt together four times. Beat the butter and sugar in a bowl until light and fluffy. Add the eggs, one at a time, beating well after each addition. Beat in the dry ingredients alternately with the milk. Beat in the vanilla and almond extract. Pour into two greased and floured 9-inch cake pans or one greased and floured tube pan. Bake at 350 degrees for 30 minutes for the cake pans or 1 hour for the tube pan. Cool in the pans for 10 minutes. Remove to a wire rack to cool completely.

Serves 8 to 10

Chocolate Syrup Cake

CAKE
1 cup all-purpose flour
1 teaspoon baking powder
Pinch of salt
1/2 cup (1 stick) butter, softened
1 cup sugar
4 eggs
1 (16-ounce) can chocolate syrup

CHOCOLATE ICING
1/2 cup (1 stick) butter
1/3 cup evaporated milk
1 cup sugar
1 cup (6 ounces) chocolate chips

For the cake, sift the flour, baking powder and salt together. Beat the butter and sugar in a bowl until light and fluffy. Add the eggs, one at a time, beating well after each addition. Beat in the dry ingredients alternately with the chocolate syrup. Pour into a greased and floured 9×13-inch baking pan. Bake at 350 degrees for 25 to 35 minutes. Remove to a wire rack to cool completely.

For the icing, combine the butter, evaporated milk and sugar in a saucepan. Cook for 3 minutes, stirring constantly. Remove from the heat and add the chocolate chips. Stir until the chocolate is melted. Pour over the cake and spread evenly. This cake keeps well and is best made one day ahead.

Serves 15

Mystery Mocha Cake

1 cup cake flour, or 1 cup minus 2 tablespoons all-purpose flour
3/4 cup granulated sugar
2 teaspoons baking powder
1/8 teaspoon salt
1 ounce unsweetened chocolate
2 tablespoons butter
1/2 cup milk
1 teaspoon vanilla extract
1/2 cup packed light brown sugar
1/2 cup granulated sugar
1/4 cup baking cocoa
1 cup brewed coffee, chilled

Sift the flour, 3/4 cup granulated sugar, baking powder and salt into a bowl. Melt the chocolate and butter together in a saucepan over low heat. Add to the dry ingredients and mix well. Stir in the milk and vanilla; the batter will be thick. Pour into a greased 8×8-inch or 9×9-inch baking pan. Combine the brown sugar, 1/2 cup granulated sugar and the baking cocoa in a bowl and mix well. Sprinkle over the batter. Pour the coffee evenly over the top. Bake at 350 degrees for 35 to 40 minutes. Remove to a wire rack to cool. Turn over each piece as it is served so the "mystery" icing appears on top of the cake. Serve warm or at room temperature with whipped cream or ice cream.

Serves 6 to 8

Pumpkin Cake Squares

CAKE
2 cups all-purpose flour
2 teaspoons baking powder
1 teaspoon salt
1 teaspoon ground cinnamon
1/2 teaspoon ginger
1/2 teaspoon nutmeg
1 cup golden raisins
1 cup pecan pieces
4 eggs
1 3/4 cups sugar
1 cup vegetable oil
1 (16-ounce) can pumpkin

ORANGE CREAM CHEESE FROSTING
6 ounces cream cheese, softened
5 1/3 tablespoons butter, softened
1 (16-ounce) package confectioners' sugar
1 tablespoon grated orange zest
4 teaspoons orange juice

For the cake, sift the flour, baking powder, salt, cinnamon, ginger and nutmeg into a bowl. Add the raisins and pecans and toss well. Beat the eggs in a large bowl with an electric mixer until frothy. Add the sugar and beat for 2 minutes. Beat in the oil and pumpkin. Add the dry ingredients, folding just until moistened; do not overmix. Pour into a greased and floured 9×13-inch baking pan. Bake at 350 degrees for 30 to 40 minutes or until the cake tests done. Remove to a wire rack to cool completely.

For the frosting, beat the cream cheese and butter in a bowl with an electric mixer until light and fluffy. Beat in the confectioners' sugar, orange zest and orange juice and beat for 1 1/2 minutes. Spread over the cooled cake. This cake is delicious even without the frosting.

Makes 2 dozen squares

Almond Crisps

2 cups all-purpose flour
Pinch of salt
3/4 cup (1 1/2 sticks) butter, softened
2 cups sugar
1/2 teaspoon grated lemon zest
1 egg
2 teaspoons vanilla extract
1 cup sliced almonds

Mix the flour and salt together. Beat the butter and sugar in a bowl until light and fluffy. Beat in the lemon zest, egg and vanilla. Beat in the dry ingredients. Stir in the almonds. Spread into a nonstick 9×13-inch baking pan. Bake at 350 degrees for 25 to 30 minutes. Cool in the pan for 5 minutes. Cut into 1×3-inch bars and cool in the pan for 10 minutes. Remove the bars to a wire rack to cool completely.

Makes 3 dozen bars

Orange Sticks

1 cup sugar
1 cup (2 sticks) butter, softened
Grated zest of 2 oranges
1 loaf sandwich bread, crusts removed

Beat the sugar and butter in a bowl until light and fluffy. Stir in the orange zest. Spread over both sides of the bread slices and cut each slice into 6 sticks. Arrange the sticks on a nonstick baking sheet. Bake at 250 degrees for 45 minutes. Turn the sticks over and bake for 15 minutes longer. Remove the sticks to a wire rack to cool completely. Store in an airtight container.

Makes about 6 dozen sticks

Chapel Hill Brownies

1 package brownie mix, prepared according to the package directions
1 cup chopped pecans
2 cups graham cracker crumbs
1 (14-ounce) can sweetened condensed milk
1 (16-ounce) package confectioners' sugar
1/4 cup (1/2 stick) butter, softened
1 teaspoon vanilla extract
5 tablespoons milk
2 tablespoons butter
2 ounces unsweetened chocolate, or
    1/4 cup semisweet chocolate chips

Spread the brownie batter in a nonstick 9×13-inch baking pan. Sprinkle the pecans over the top. Combine the graham cracker crumbs and sweetened condensed milk in a bowl and mix well. Drop by spoonfuls over the batter to cover the entire surface. Bake at 350 degrees for 30 minutes or until the brownies test done. Remove to a wire rack to cool completely. Combine the confectioners' sugar, 1/4 cup butter, the vanilla and milk in a bowl and mix well. Spread over the cooled brownies. Melt 2 tablespoons butter and chocolate in a saucepan over low heat. Spread evenly over the frosting layer. Cool and cut into squares. If you wish to drizzle the chocolate glaze rather than spread it, use chocolate chips as this makes it thicker and easier to drizzle.

Makes 2 to 2 1/2 dozen squares

Mexican-Style Pecan Chocolate Squares

CRUST
3/4 cup (1 1/2 sticks) chilled unsalted butter,
  cut into 1/2-inch pieces
2 cups all-purpose flour
1/2 cup packed light brown sugar
2 teaspoons ground cinnamon
1/2 teaspoon salt
2 ounces grated bittersweet chocolate
  (scant 1/2 cup)

TOPPING
1/2 cup (1 stick) unsalted butter
1 cup packed dark brown sugar
1/3 cup honey
2 tablespoons heavy cream or fat-free half-and-half
1/2 teaspoon salt
3 cups (10 ounces) toasted pecans,
  coarsely chopped in a food processor

For the crust, combine the butter, flour, brown sugar, cinnamon and salt in a food processor. Pulse about 20 times or until well mixed. Pat into a nonstick 9×9-inch baking pan. Bake at 350 degrees for 25 minutes or until firm and light brown. Sprinkle the chocolate evenly over the baked crust and set aside.

For the topping, melt the butter in a saucepan. Stir in the brown sugar, honey, cream and salt. Simmer for 1 minute, stirring occasionally. Stir in the pecans. Pour over the crust and spread evenly. Bake at 350 degrees for 16 to 20 minutes or until bubbly. Remove to a wire rack to cool completely. Cut into 1-inch squares. Tightly covered bars will keep for 5 days or they may be frozen.

Makes 32 squares

Chocolate Toffee Bars

1/2 cup (1 stick) butter, melted
13/4 cups crushed chocolate teddy bear graham crackers
11/4 cups almond brickle bits
6 (1-ounce) English toffee candy bars, crushed
1 cup (6 ounces) semisweet chocolate chips
1 cup chopped pecans
1/2 cup chopped walnuts
1 (14-ounce) can sweetened condensed milk

Line a 9×13-inch baking pan with foil, allowing the foil to extend over the edges of the pan. Pour the melted butter evenly into the pan. Sprinkle the graham cracker crumbs evenly over the butter and press down. Bake at 325 degrees for 5 minutes. Sprinkle with the brickle bits and then with the crushed toffee bars. Sprinkle with the chocolate chips. Sprinkle with the pecans and walnuts and press down. Pour the sweetened condensed milk evenly over the top. Bake for 30 minutes or until the edges are light brown. Remove to a wire rack to cool completely. Lift out of the pan by the foil edges and cut into bars. These bars freeze well.

Makes 2 dozen bars

Frangelico Squares

3/4 cup (1 1/2 sticks) plus 3 tablespoons
   unsalted butter, softened
1/4 cup granulated sugar
3 cups all-purpose flour
4 eggs
2 3/4 cups packed brown sugar
1/3 cup all-purpose flour
1 teaspoon baking powder
2 cups walnuts
1 cup flaked coconut
2 tablespoons Frangelico liqueur
1/4 cup (1/2 stick) unsalted butter, softened
2 1/2 cups sifted confectioners' sugar
2 tablespoons Frangelico liqueur

Beat 3/4 cup plus 3 tablespoons butter and granulated sugar in a bowl until light
and fluffy. Add 3 cups flour and mix until crumbly. Press into a greased 10×15-inch
baking pan. Bake at 350 degrees for 20 minutes or until golden brown. Beat the eggs
in a bowl with an electric mixer until frothy. Add the brown sugar and beat until thick.
Sift 1/3 cup flour and baking powder together. Stir into the egg mixture. Stir in the
walnuts and coconut. Stir in 2 tablespoons liqueur. Spread over the baked base. Bake at
350 degrees for 35 to 45 minutes. Remove to a wire rack to cool completely. Beat
1/4 cup butter and confectioners' sugar in a bowl until light and fluffy. Add 2 tablespoons
liqueur and beat to a spreading consistency. Spread over the cooled bars. Chill for
30 minutes. Cut into bars.

Makes 2 dozen bars

 When cooking with liqueurs, consider purchasing miniature bottles from the
liquor store.

Cranberry Orange Drop Cookies

2 cups packed sweetened dried cranberries
   (about 10 ounces)
1/3 cup orange juice
2 cups all-purpose flour
1 teaspoon baking powder
1 teaspoon ground cinnamon
3/4 teaspoon ginger
1/4 teaspoon baking soda
1/4 teaspoon salt
1 cup (2 sticks) unsalted butter, softened
1 cup packed light brown sugar
1 egg
1 tablespoon minced fresh ginger
2 teaspoons vanilla extract
1 1/2 teaspoons grated orange zest
3/4 cup chopped walnuts or pecans
3/4 cup chopped unsalted natural pistachios
1/2 cup coarsely chopped fresh or frozen cranberries

Combine the sweetened dried cranberries and orange juice in a bowl. Let stand for
30 minutes or until the cranberries have softened slightly. Whisk the flour, baking powder,
cinnamon, ginger, baking soda and salt in a bowl. Beat the butter and brown sugar in
a bowl with an electric mixer until light and fluffy. Add the egg, ginger, vanilla and
orange zest and beat for 2 minutes. Add the flour mixture and beat well. Stir in the
walnuts, pistachios, fresh cranberries and dried cranberries with orange juice. Drop by
spoonfuls onto a buttered baking sheet or parchment-lined baking sheet. Bake, one
sheet at a time, at 350 degrees for 18 minutes or until golden brown and firm. Cool
on the baking sheet for 5 minutes. Remove to a wire rack to cool completely. Bake for
12 minutes if making smaller cookies.

Makes about 4 dozen cookies

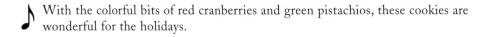 With the colorful bits of red cranberries and green pistachios, these cookies are
wonderful for the holidays.

Tortilla Flats

¹/2 cup (1 stick) unsalted butter, softened
¹/2 cup shortening
2 cups packed light brown sugar
1 egg
2 teaspoons ground cinnamon
1 teaspoon vanilla extract
¹/2 teaspoon baking soda
¹/4 teaspoon salt
1¹/2 cups rolled oats, lightly toasted
1¹/2 cups coarsely ground plain tortilla chips
1¹/4 cups all-purpose flour
¹/2 cup chopped pecans or pine nuts, toasted

Beat the butter, shortening and brown sugar in a bowl with an electric mixer until light and fluffy. Add the egg, cinnamon, vanilla, baking soda and salt and beat well. Stir in the oats. Add the tortilla chips, flour and pecans and mix well. Drop by heaping tablespoons 2 inches apart onto a greased and floured baking sheet. Flatten the cookies to 2-inch rounds with the bottom of a glass dipped in sugar. Bake at 350 degrees for 8 to 9 minutes. Cool on the baking sheet for 2 to 3 minutes. Remove to a wire rack to cool completely. Store in an airtight container. Bake for 7 to 8 minutes if making smaller cookies.

Makes 4¹/2 dozen cookies

Chocolate Chess Pie with Meringue

5 tablespoons baking cocoa
1 tablespoon all-purpose flour
1 1/2 cups sugar
2 eggs, beaten
1/2 cup milk
1 teaspoon vanilla extract

1/2 cup (1 stick) butter, melted
1 unbaked (9-inch) pie shell
4 egg whites, at room temperature
1/4 teaspoon cream of tartar
1/2 cup sugar

Combine the baking cocoa, flour, 1 1/2 cups sugar, the eggs, milk, vanilla and melted butter in a bowl and mix well. Pour into the pie shell. Bake at 400 degrees for 10 minutes. Reduce the heat to 325 degrees and bake for 30 minutes longer. Beat the egg whites and cream of tartar in a bowl with an electric mixer at medium speed until soft peaks form. Beat in 1/2 cup sugar, 2 tablespoons at a time and beat until soft peaks form. Spread over the hot filling, sealing to the edge. Bake at 400 degrees for 7 to 9 minutes or until golden brown and the egg white is cooked through. Remove to a wire rack to cool for at least 1 hour.

Serves 8

Sherried Walnut Pie

1/4 cup (1/2 stick) butter or margarine
2 tablespoons all-purpose flour
1/2 cup dark corn syrup
1/3 cup amontillado sherry

1 cup sugar
3 eggs
1 cup walnuts, coarsely chopped
1 unbaked (9-inch) pie shell

Melt the butter in a saucepan. Stir in the flour, corn syrup, sherry and sugar. Bring to a boil, stirring constantly. Remove from the heat and let cool slightly. Whisk the eggs in a bowl. Whisk in the hot sherry mixture gradually. Stir in the walnuts. Pour into the pie shell. Bake at 375 degrees for 45 minutes or until firm. Remove to a wire rack. Serve warm or chilled with ice cream or whipped cream.

Serves 8

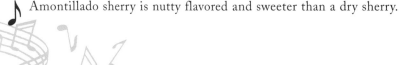
Amontillado sherry is nutty flavored and sweeter than a dry sherry.

Blueberry Lemon Curd Tart

1/2 cup (1 stick) unsalted butter
1/2 cup sugar
Grated zest of 1 large or 2 small lemons
6 tablespoons fresh lemon juice
3 eggs
1 baked (9-inch) tart shell
2 cups fresh blueberries

Combine the butter, sugar, lemon zest and lemon juice in a 4-cup glass measuring cup. Microwave, loosely covered with plastic wrap, on High for 4 minutes. Stir well. Whisk the eggs lightly in a bowl. Whisk in one-fourth of the hot lemon mixture. Whisk the eggs back into the lemon mixture. Microwave, uncovered, on High for 2 minutes. Whisk until smooth. Microwave on High for 2 minutes longer. Pour into a food processor and process until smooth. Pour into a bowl and let cool. Pour the cooled lemon curd into the tart shell and top with the blueberries.

Serves 8

Rustic Fruit Tart

1 (2-crust) refrigerator pie pastry
4 to 6 cups sliced fresh peaches
1 cup fresh blueberries
1/4 cup sugar
Dash of freshly grated nutmeg
2 tablespoons apricot preserves, heated
1 tablespoon sugar

Line two 10×15-inch baking pans with baking parchment paper. Roll out each pie pastry on the parchment paper to a 12-inch circle. Combine the peaches, blueberries, 1/4 cup sugar and nutmeg in a bowl and mix well. Spread half the fruit mixture over each pastry, leaving a 3-inch border. Fold the edges of the pastry in, pressing to seal. Brush equal portions of the apricot preserves over the fruit and pastry of each tart. Bake at 425 degrees for 10 minutes. Reduce the heat to 350 degrees and bake for 20 minutes longer. Sprinkle each warm tart with equal portions of the 1 tablespoon sugar.

Serves 16

Fresh Fruit Tart

CRUST
2 cups ground chocolate cookies, gingersnap cookies or butter cookies
  (about 38 cookies)
2 tablespoons sugar
5 1/3 tablespoons butter, softened

FILLING
8 ounces cream cheese, softened
1/4 cup sugar
2 teaspoons lemon juice
1/2 cup cream or heavy cream
Assorted fresh fruit such as strawberries, blueberries,
  kiwifruit, orange sections and seedless red or green grapes
1/4 cup apricot preserves
1 tablespoon water or brandy

For the crust, combine the cookie crumbs and sugar in a bowl and mix well. Cut in the butter with a pastry blender or fork until crumbly. Press over the bottom and up the side of a 10-inch springform pan. Bake at 350 degrees for 8 minutes or until light brown. Remove to a wire rack to cool completely.

For the filling, beat the cream cheese, sugar and lemon juice in a bowl with an electric mixer until light and fluffy. Add the cream and beat at high speed until light and fluffy. Spread over the cooled crust. Chill for several hours. Arrange the fruit on top of the cream cheese mixture. Combine the preserves and water in a small saucepan. Bring to a boil, stirring frequently. Strain through a wire mesh strainer into a bowl. Brush over the fruit. Loosen from the side of the pan with a sharp knife and remove the side. For a lighter version, use 1 cup low-fat lemon yogurt instead of the cream cheese, sugar, lemon juice and cream.

Serves 8

Almond Torte

3/4 cup (1¹/2 sticks) butter, softened
1¹/2 cups sugar
2 eggs
1¹/2 cups all-purpose flour
2 teaspoons almond extract
Pinch of salt
¹/4 cup sliced almonds
2 tablespoons sugar

Beat the butter, 1¹/2 cups sugar and the eggs in a bowl until light and fluffy. Beat in the flour, almond extract and salt. Pour into a greased 9- or 10-inch springform pan and smooth the top of the batter. Sprinkle with the almonds and 2 tablespoons sugar. Bake at 350 degrees for 30 to 40 minutes or until golden brown. Remove to a wire rack to cool completely. Loosen from the side of the pan with a sharp knife and remove the side. Cut into small wedges and serve. Use colored sugar instead of plain sugar on the top for holidays and special occasions.

Serves 16

Butter Pecan Cheesecake

CRUST
1 1/2 cups graham cracker crumbs
1/3 cup sugar
1/2 cup finely chopped pecans
5 1/3 tablespoons butter or margarine, melted

FILLING
24 ounces cream cheese, softened
1 1/2 cups sugar
3 eggs
2 cups sour cream
1 teaspoon vanilla extract
1/2 teaspoon butter flavoring
1 cup finely chopped pecans, toasted

For the crust, combine the graham cracker crumbs, sugar, pecans and melted butter in a bowl and mix well. Remove and reserve 1/3 cup of the mixture. Press the remaining mixture over the bottom of a 9-inch springform pan.

For the filling, beat the cream cheese in a bowl with an electric mixer until light and fluffy. Beat in the sugar gradually. Add the eggs, one at a time, beating well after each addition. Beat in the sour cream, vanilla and butter flavoring. Stir in the pecans. Pour into the prepared crust. Sprinkle with the reserved crumb mixture. Bake at 475 degrees for 10 minutes. Reduce the heat to 350 degrees and bake for 50 minutes longer. Remove to a wire rack to cool completely. Chill, covered, until cold. Loosen from the side of the pan with a sharp knife and remove the side.

Serves 8

Lime Cheesecake

CRUST
1 1/2 cups graham cracker crumbs
2 tablespoons sugar
6 tablespoons butter, melted and cooled

FILLING
20 ounces cream cheese, softened
3/4 cup sugar
1 cup sour cream
3 tablespoons all-purpose flour
3 eggs
3/4 cup lime juice
1 teaspoon vanilla extract

For the crust, combine the graham cracker crumbs and sugar in a bowl and mix well. Add the melted butter and mix well. Press over the bottom of a greased 10-inch springform pan. Bake on the center rack of the oven at 350 degrees for 8 minutes. Remove to a wire rack to cool completely.

For the filling, beat the cream cheese and sugar in a bowl with an electric mixer until light and fluffy. Beat in the sour cream and flour. Add the eggs, one at a time, beating well after each addition. Add the lime juice and vanilla and beat until smooth. Pour into the baked crust. Bake on the center rack of the oven at 375 degrees for 15 minutes. Reduce the heat to 250 degrees and bake for 50 to 55 minutes longer or until the center is barely set. Remove to a wire rack to cool completely. Chill, covered, overnight. Loosen from the side of the pan with a sharp knife and remove the side. Serve garnished with whipped cream, lime slices and mint sprigs. Crushed chocolate cookies may be used instead of graham cracker crumbs.

Serves 8

Chocolate Crème Brûlée

1 cup cream or heavy cream
1/2 vanilla bean, split lengthwise
2 ounces semisweet chocolate, coarsely chopped
2 egg yolks
3 tablespoons superfine sugar
Pinch of salt
2 tablespoons superfine sugar

Combine the cream and vanilla bean in a saucepan. Bring to a simmer over medium heat. Remove from the heat and remove the vanilla bean. Scrape the seeds from the vanilla bean into the hot cream and discard the vanilla bean. Add the chocolate to the hot cream and stir until the chocolate is melted. Whisk the egg yolks, 3 tablespoons sugar and salt in a bowl until thick and creamy. Whisk in the warm cream mixture slowly. Pour into two 6-ounce ramekins. Place the ramekins in a baking pan lined with a kitchen towel. Add enough boiling water to the larger pan to come halfway up the sides of the ramekins. Cover loosely with foil. Bake at 325 degrees for 20 to 25 minutes or until the edges are set and centers wiggle when shaken. Remove the ramekins to a wire rack and let cool for 1 hour. Chill, covered, for 3 hours to overnight. Sprinkle equal amounts of the 2 tablespoons sugar over each ramekin. Place under a broiler for 1 to 2 minutes or until the sugar is melted and caramelized. Serve immediately.

Serves 2

Chocolate Mousse

1 tablespoon butter
3 ounces unsweetened chocolate
2 egg whites
1/4 cup sugar
2 egg yolks
1/4 cup sugar
2 teaspoons dark rum
1 teaspoon strong brewed coffee, chilled
1 cup heavy whipping cream, whipped

Melt the butter and chocolate in a small heavy saucepan over low heat. Stir until smooth and remove from the heat. Beat the egg whites in a small bowl with an electric mixer until foamy. Beat in 1/4 cup sugar gradually and beat until stiff. Beat the egg yolks and 1/4 cup sugar in a large bowl until pale yellow. Beat in the rum and coffee. Fold in the chocolate mixture, egg white mixture and whipped cream just until combined. Spoon into 4 serving dishes. Chill, covered, for several hours to overnight.

Serves 4

Peach Berry Cobbler

FRUIT
1/4 cup granulated sugar
1/4 cup packed brown sugar
1 tablespoon cornstarch
1/2 cup water
1 tablespoon lemon juice
2 cups sliced fresh peaches (about 4 peaches)
1 cup fresh blueberries

TOPPING
1 cup all-purpose flour
1/2 cup sugar
1 1/2 teaspoons baking powder
1/2 teaspoon salt
1/2 cup milk
1/4 cup (1/2 stick) butter, softened
2 tablespoons sugar
1/4 teaspoon nutmeg

For the fruit, combine the granulated sugar, brown sugar, cornstarch and water in a saucepan. Cook over medium heat until thickened, stirring constantly. Remove from the heat and stir in the lemon juice, peaches and blueberries. Pour into a 2-quart baking dish.

For the topping, sift the flour, 1/2 cup sugar, the baking powder and salt into a bowl. Add the milk and butter and beat until smooth. Spoon evenly over the fruit. Mix 2 tablespoons sugar and nutmeg in a small bowl. Sprinkle over the batter. Bake at 375 degrees for 40 to 45 minutes. Remove to a wire rack to cool. Frozen fruit may be used instead of fresh fruit but omit the 1/2 cup sugar if the frozen fruit is sweetened.

Serves 6 to 8

Bottoms-Up Blueberry Cobbler

6 tablespoons unsalted butter
1 cup all-purpose flour
2 teaspoons baking powder
1/2 teaspoon salt
1/2 teaspoon freshly grated nutmeg
Dash of ground cinnamon (optional)
1 cup sugar
2/3 cup milk
2 cups fresh blueberries

Melt the butter in an 8×8-inch baking pan in the oven. Sift the flour, baking powder, salt, nutmeg and cinnamon into a bowl. Stir in the sugar. Whisk in the milk just until combined. Pour evenly over the melted butter in the baking pan; do not stir. Sprinkle the blueberries over the top. Bake on the center rack of the oven at 375 degrees for 40 minutes or until golden brown and the blueberries are juicy. Serve warm or at room temperature with whipped cream or ice cream.

Serves 6 to 8

♪ Fresh ground nutmeg is far superior to packaged. Purchase a whole nutmeg seed and grate as needed. Store whole seed in a glass jar with a tight-fitting lid.

Scottish Sticky Toffee Pudding

PUDDING
18 dates, chopped
1/2 teaspoon baking soda
1 cup boiling water
1/4 cup (1/2 stick) butter, softened
1 cup Demerara sugar or turbinado sugar
1 egg
2 cups self-rising flour

SAUCE
3 tablespoons butter
1 1/3 cups packed brown sugar
1/2 scant cup cream or heavy cream

For the pudding, combine the dates and baking soda in a bowl. Add the boiling water and let stand until the dates have softened. Beat the butter and Demerara sugar in a bowl until light and fluffy. Beat in the egg. Add the flour and mix well; the batter will be stiff. Stir in the date mixture. Pour into a greased 9×9-inch baking pan. Bake at 350 degrees for 35 to 40 minutes or until golden brown.

For the sauce, combine the butter, brown sugar and cream in a saucepan. Bring to a boil and cook until thickened. Pour evenly over the hot cake. Place under the broiler for 1 minute or until bubbly. Remove from the oven and let stand for 15 to 20 minutes. Serve warm or at room temperature garnished with whipped cream. This is the "original" recipe from the Udney Arms Hotel in Scotland.

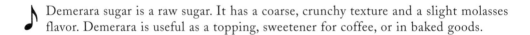 Demerara sugar is a raw sugar. It has a coarse, crunchy texture and a slight molasses flavor. Demerara is useful as a topping, sweetener for coffee, or in baked goods.

White Chocolate Almond Bread Pudding

2 cups cream or heavy cream
1 cup packed brown sugar
8 ounces white chocolate
3 to 4 cups cubed French bread (1-inch cubes)
3 eggs
1 cup almonds, chopped
Caramel ice cream topping
Whipped cream

Heat the cream in a heavy saucepan over medium-high heat. Add the brown sugar and cook until the sugar is melted, stirring constantly. Add the chocolate and cook until the chocolate is melted, stirring constantly. Reduce the heat to low. Stir in enough of the bread so that a small amount of liquid remains. Turn off the heat and let stand for 20 minutes, stirring every 5 minutes. Add the eggs, one at a time, mixing well after each addition. Stir in the almonds. Spoon into ramekins and place on a baking sheet or spoon into nonstick muffin cups. Bake at 350 degrees for 20 to 25 minutes or until set. Remove to a wire rack and let cool until able to handle. Remove from the ramekins. Spoon caramel topping onto serving plates. Place one pudding on each plate and top with whipped cream. These can be made one day ahead. Chill, covered. Warm in the oven prior to serving.

Serves 6 to 8

Raspberry Flambé

1 (10-ounce) package frozen raspberries,
   thawed, drained and juice reserved
1/2 cup orange juice
1 tablespoon cornstarch
1/3 cup brandy
Vanilla ice cream

Mix the reserved raspberry juice, orange juice and cornstarch in a saucepan. Bring to a boil, stirring constantly. Cook for 2 to 3 minutes, stirring constantly. Stir in the raspberries gently. Heat the brandy in a small saucepan until bubbles begin to form around the edge. Ignite the brandy with a long match and carefully pour over the raspberry mixture. Spoon the sauce carefully over ice cream in heatproof serving dishes.

Serves 6 to 8

Chocolate Chip Cheese Ball

1/2 cup (1 stick) butter, softened
8 ounces cream cheese, softened
1/2 teaspoon vanilla extract
3/4 cup confectioners' sugar
2 tablespoons brown sugar
3/4 cup miniature chocolate chips
Chopped pecans

Beat the butter, cream cheese and vanilla in a bowl until smooth. Mix the confectioners' sugar and brown sugar in a bowl. Add to the cream cheese mixture and mix well. Stir in the chocolate chips. Chill, covered, for 2 to 3 hours. Shape into a ball and roll in the pecans. Serve with chocolate teddy bear graham crackers. This can be served as an appetizer or dessert. Children love it.

Serves 24

Mint Ice Cream Sandwiches

1 (2-layer) package devil's food cake mix
1/2 cup (1 stick) butter, softened
1/4 cup all-purpose flour
2 eggs
1 quart mint chocolate chip ice cream, slightly softened

Combine the cake mix, butter, flour and eggs in a bowl and mix well. Form into twenty balls, each about 1 1/2 tablespoons. Place the balls on a nonstick baking sheet and press to flatten. Bake at 350 degrees for 8 minutes; the cookies will be soft. Cool on the baking sheet for 5 minutes. Remove to a wire rack to cool completely. Spread about 1/3 cup ice cream over each of 10 cookies. Top with the remaining cookies. Freeze, covered, until firm. You may also use other flavors of ice cream.

Serves 10

♪ The easiest way to flatten the cookies is to use the bottom of a glass dipped in sugar, baking cocoa or hot chocolate mix.

Frozen Strawberry Cream

1 cup all-purpose flour
1/4 cup packed brown sugar
1/2 cup chopped nuts
1/2 cup (1 stick) butter, melted
2 egg whites

1 cup sugar
2 cups frozen strawberries, thawed
2 tablespoons lemon juice
1 cup heavy whipping cream, whipped

Combine the flour, brown sugar, nuts and melted butter in a bowl and mix well. Spread in a 9×13-inch baking dish. Bake at 350 degrees for 20 minutes, stirring occasionally. Remove to a wire rack and let cool completely. Beat the eggs whites in a large bowl with an electric mixer until stiff. Beat in the sugar gradually. Beat in the strawberries and lemon juice. Beat at medium speed for 10 minutes. Fold in the whipped cream. Spread over the crumb layer in the baking dish. Freeze, covered, for at least 6 hours. Cut into squares and serve with additional whipped cream and fresh strawberries.

Serves 18

♪ If you are concerned about using raw eggs, use an equivalent amount of pasteurized egg whites.

Blood Orange Sorbet

1 scant cup superfine sugar
6 tablespoons water
Juice of 5 blood oranges

Juice of 2 lemons
Fresh orange juice
Orange liqueur (optional)

Cook the sugar and water in a saucepan until the sugar is dissolved, stirring constantly. Bring to a boil and boil for 3 minutes or until syrupy. Combine the blood orange juice and lemon juice in a 4-cup measuring cup. Stir in the sugar syrup. Add enough orange juice or orange juice plus orange liqueur to make 4 cups. Pour into an ice cream freezer container. Freeze using the manufacturer's directions. Serve immediately or remove to an airtight container and freeze until ready to serve. Scoop into serving glasses, garnish with mint sprigs and drizzle with orange liqueur. Serve with dark chocolate wafer cookies.

Serves 6

Balsamic Strawberry Sauce

2 tablespoons brown sugar
2 tablespoons balsamic vinegar
1/8 teaspoon nutmeg
3 cups sliced strawberries

Combine the brown sugar, vinegar and nutmeg in a saucepan. Bring to a simmer over medium-low heat, stirring frequently. Cook for 2 minutes or until slightly thickened, stirring frequently. Stir in the strawberries and remove from the heat. Let stand for 5 minutes. Serve over frozen yogurt or ice cream. Stirring the strawberries in at the end of cooking helps retain their shape.

Serves 7

Hot Fudge Sauce

1/2 cup (1 stick) butter
4 ounces unsweetened chocolate
2 cups sugar
1 (12-ounce) can evaporated milk
1 teaspoon vanilla extract
Dash of salt

Combine the butter and chocolate in the top of a double boiler and place over simmering water. Cook until melted, stirring often. Stir in the sugar. Stir in the evaporated milk, vanilla and salt. Cook until thick, stirring frequently. Remove to a jar with a tight-fitting lid. Store in the refrigerator.

Serves 10

Index

Contributors

The Greensboro Symphony Guild and cookbook committee would like
to express their appreciation to everyone who submitted a recipe.
Many hundreds of recipes were received, but unfortunately we were unable
to include them all. The contributors' names are included in the list below.
We regret if anyone's name has inadvertently been overlooked.

Jane Adair
Jackie Adams
Karen Andersen
Joanne Anderson
Carol Andresen
Kay Arthur
Brenda Asbury
Jill Auslander
Brenda Barnes
Vivien Bauman
Nan Bayersdorfer
Lena Baynes
Shari Beavers
Elizabeth Bell
Anne Bodner
Susan Bohn
Lib Boone
Sandy Boulden
Barbara Braswell
Teresa Brenholdt
Becky Brown
Mary Ellen Burke
Carol Burklin
Maureen Burns
Kathy Busby
Martha Chandler
Vito Ciccone

Louann Clarke
Marsha Cole
Marilyn Cotten
Pat Cross
Faye Cross
Jane Curtis
Anne Daniel
Pam Drag
Rachel Dunn
Margaret Faison
Carolyn Fancett
Nan Faram
Peggy Follin
Judy Foran
Rachel Galyon
Susan Gray
Ginger Griffin
Dolly Guertin
Judy Guidone
Peggy Hamilton
Kim Harrison
Miriam Harrison
Barbara Hemphill
Jessica Herman
Donna Hodgman
Linda Hofmann
Antoinette Horan

Myra Hinote
Sandra Jameson
Maxine Johnson
Nancy Jones
Cathy Kennedy
Jo Kennedy
Gail Kinser
Harriette Knox
Judy Lambeth
Mary Lipiah
Kim Littrell
Mary Lysiak
Natalie Mapou
Esther Mathews
John Matthews
Sandy McCall
Fray Metcalfe
Nancy Michaud
Carole Moore
Cotten Moring
Sharon Novak
Denise Oliphant
Louise O'Shea
Alice Pearce
Jo Phillips
Rosemary Reed
Catherine Rice

Donna Richardson
Carla Robinson
Mary Rogg
Margaret Rubiera
Marnie Ruskin
Nell Schopp
Pat Sevier
Dianne Shope
Martha Siler
Dinny Sisley
Jonathan Smith
Joyce Somers
Valerie Sutton
Ellen Taft
Peggy Tager
Melissa Tankersley
Sandy Thompson
Suzanne Tritch
JW Turner
Marilyn Tyson
Frances Vinoski
Anne Wade
Suzy Walker
Sandy Weston
Carolyn Witman
Darlene Young

Recipes of Note

A COLLECTION OF RECIPES FROM
THE GREENSBORO SYMPHONY GUILD
P.O. BOX 29224
GREENSBORO, NORTH CAROLINA 27429-9224
WWW.GSOGUILD.ORG

YOUR ORDER	QTY	TOTAL
Recipes of Note at $23.95 per book		$
North Carolina residents add 7% sales tax		$
Shipping and handling at $5.50 per book		$
TOTAL		$

Please make check payable to GREENSBORO SYMPHONY GUILD.

Name

Street Address

City   State   Zip

Telephone   E-mail Address

Photocopies will be accepted.